"The inspirational story of The Gambler's Mission, as told by Adam Winters, is ever so much more than a biography of the life and ministry of Steve Holcombe, and even more than a history of the Louisville Rescue Mission, as important as these things may be. Rather, this carefully-written work points to the power and life-changing work of the gospel of Jesus Christ and its influence on real people and their families. It is the story of the importance of benevolence ministry along with the social and cultural aspects of the life of the church. The Gambler's Mission points readers to what is involved in living out the 'salt and light' implications of the teachings of Jesus, what the Book of James refers to as 'pure and undefiled religion.' It is a joy to commend this outstanding work by Adam Winters."

David S. Dockery,
President, Trinity International University

—

"There are many conversations being had about mercy ministry and caring for the poor, but few models exist, especially those that have stood the test of time doing the work long before it became a trend in the modern church. This is one of many reasons why you hold an absolute gem in your hand! This historical account of the long, faithful history of the Louisville Rescue Mission is not only the definitive historical work on this amazing mission, but acts as a tested model for those trying to reach the homeless and hurting with the gospel today. The powerful story of Steve Holcombe's conversion and the storytelling abilities of this careful historian are worth the price of the book alone. Read this book and be amazed at what the power of Christ can do when the unchanging gospel remains central in a man's life and in his ministry."

Brian Croft
Pastor, Auburndale Baptist Church; Founder, Practical Shepherding

—

"What a compelling story is the life of Steve Holcombe and the Louisville Rescue Mission! Adam Winters brings this story to life detailing the grace of God in converting sinners and inspiring believers to care for those in need. This is an encouraging account demonstrating how faithful gospel preaching and care for those in need can and should go hand in hand. I also appreciated how Winters regularly pointed out the importance of soul care in ministry. This book deserves a wide reading."

Ray Van Neste
Professor, Union University

—

"I have to confess that I was not immediately excited about reading a history of a local city ministry but this book proved to be an unexpected delight. I am so glad that the powerful story of Steve Holcombe's conversion has been told in such an engaging and thoughtful way. More than a simple retelling of the story of one man's radical conversion, Winters also lays out for us the story of the Louisville Rescue Mission in a way that casts a helpful vision for those doing similar work in other contexts. He reminds us of the call to biblical fidelity, God centered confidence, and gospel partnerships. This little book has served to stir my heart and encourage me to press on in the work of ministering to the poor and needy."

Matthew Spandler-Davison
Executive Director, 20 Schemes

—

"Adam's book is a compelling history and engagingly written story about a ministry that has impacted the souls of men for well over a century. It speaks to the power of one man's broken journey, his vision of hope and God's redemptive mercies to change the destiny of thousands. It is a gripping story of the love of Christ in action."

Rob Gibson
Pastor, Christ Church at Goshen, KY; Former Chairman of the Board, LRM

The
GAMBLER'S
MISSION

Steve P. Holcombe and the
Heritage of the Louisville Rescue Mission

BY ADAM GARLAND WINTERS

LOUISVILLE
Rescue Mission

The Gambler's Mission
Steve P. Holcombe and the Heritage of the Louisville Rescue Mission

© 2016 by Jefferson Street Baptist Center/Louisville Rescue Mission

Cover and interior design: Andrea Stember

Library of Congress Cataloging-in-Publication Data
A catalog record for this book is available from the Library of Congress.

ISBN 978-0-692-75300-2

Printed in the United States of America

*"Dedicated to those who labor,
to the heavy laden,
and to those who seek rest."*
(Matthew 11:28)

CONTENTS

FOREWORD

In the past century, numerous Evangelicals, including many Baptists, have wrestled with whether or not a commitment to preaching the gospel also entails engaging in the alleviation of social ills—such things as drug and alcohol abuse, the harmful effects of poverty, prostitution and gambling. In many respects this quandary is a result of the divide that took place in the first third of the twentieth century when, especially within Baptist and Presbyterian denominations, Fundamentalists and so-called Modernists parted company. Fundamentalists and far too many of their Evangelical heirs—though not all, it should be noted—came to the wrong conclusion that the Modernist emphasis on the social gospel must mean that it was a major cause of their catastrophic drift into theological heterodoxy. In fact, earlier generations of Evangelicals felt no such divide between evangelism and doing good works—witness the remarkable anti-slavery campaign associated with the name of William Wilberforce or the numerous Victorian Evangelical do-gooders (in the best sense of that term), men and women like Hannah More and the seventh Earl of Shaftesbury, Anthony Ashley-Cooper—or Steve P. Holcombe, the main figure of the early chapters of this fascinating study of the social impact of the gospel here in Louisville. The Louisville Rescue Mission, one of the oldest rescue missions in America, is a fabulous example of the intertwining of the gospel and the good works that ultimately issue forth whenever genuine faith in Christ is experienced.

The life of Steve Holcombe, who founded the mission, is also a great example of the way that the gospel transforms a person—in his case from a gambler and drunk to a man of God—and the enormous impact that such a transformation can have for good in a community. Adam Winters carefully traces the history of this impact over the past 135 years of the mission's existence, from its early days as part of the Methodist fold to its present place among the Baptists, and faithfully details the story of the various leaders who have been part of this great work. But whether Methodist or Baptist, the critical thing is that good has been done to the poor and downtrodden of Louisville and the gospel of Christ proclaimed to them. And it is fitting that this story be told in this centennial year of the home-going of Steve Holcombe as a celebration of the good that can flow from a single life.

Michael A.G. Haykin
Professor of Church History & Biblical Spirituality,
The Southern Baptist Theological Seminary
Louisville, Kentucky
April 2016

PREFACE AND ACKNOWLEDGMENTS

This is the story of the Louisville Rescue Mission, the oldest rescue mission in Louisville, Kentucky. It is among the oldest missions of its kind in the United States. The impetus of the original idea comes from a single individual, Steve P. Holcombe, who devoted his life to evangelizing and aiding the most destitute men of the city unlikely to frequent the existing churches of Louisville. The Louisville Rescue Mission has operated under a variety of staff and even a variety of names. Holcombe's desire for rescue ministry actually preceded the Mission's official incorporation, and for some years he ministered to the poor and needy of Louisville as the "Holcombe Mission" under support from a local Methodist church. In 1885, his ministry incorporated as the Union Gospel Mission, a non-denominational evangelical partnership. During the 1940s, the Mission came under the ownership of the Long Run Baptist Association, and it received its support from Southern Baptists. Under the Baptist banner, the Mission has operated under various designations including Central Baptist Mission, Central Baptist Chapel, Jefferson Street Baptist Chapel, the Jefferson Street Baptist Center, and its current name, adopted in 2014 as the Louisville Rescue Mission.

A renewed interest in the legacy of Steve Holcombe has motivated the creation of this history. Those who labor in the present can find inspiration from those who have left a legacy of a bountiful harvest. The Mission had not received a comprehensive history since the 1944 publication of *The Story of the Union Gospel Mission*

11

by its former superintendent Maude M. Abner. Her work still deserves appreciation, as Abner drew heavily from the Mission's official records, in addition to over a decade of personal experience in the trenches of the work. Her effort ensured the preservation of the Mission's official records during the institution's adoption by the Long Run Baptist Association. The first two chapters of this book build upon the foundation of Gross Alexander's *Steve P. Holcombe, The Converted Gambler: His Life and Work* (1888). Chapters three through six rely upon the official records of the Union Gospel Mission composed between 1885 and 1944. Chapters seven and eight make extensive usage of the minutes of the annual meetings of the Long Run Baptist Association, the Long Run Association's circular newsletters, the *Western Recorder*, and other publications produced by various entities of the Southern Baptist Convention.

The original manuscripts and materials related to the Union Gospel Mission (1885-1944) are now housed in the Archives & Special Collections of the James P. Boyce Centennial Library at The Southern Baptist Theological Seminary in Louisville, Kentucky. Additional records, correspondence, and memorabilia from the Mission's existence are housed at the Jefferson Street Baptist Community at Liberty, 800 E Liberty St, Louisville, Kentucky; I extend my thanks to Cindy J. Weber for allowing me the privilege of accessing these materials for my research and additionally for contributing some photographs for this project. I am grateful to Bryce Butler and Jesse Eubanks for permitting me to interview them regarding their involvement with the Jefferson Street Baptist Center/Louisville Rescue Mission. Cory Bledsoe, executive director of the Louisville Rescue Mission, provided photographs and collected the personal testimonials for the appendices. Teresa Gray, Public Services Archivist at Vanderbilt University, Dale Patterson, United Methodist Church Archives, and Jennifer Cole, The Filson

Historical Society, provided reference services for various historical resources.

This book is offered with the prayer that it might benefit the ongoing work of the Louisville Rescue Mission. I am honored that Dr. Michael A. G. Haykin, Professor of Church History and Biblical Spirituality at the Southern Baptist Theological Seminary, provided the foreword for the book. This publication benefited from the editorial services of RuthAnne Irvin and the graphical design talents of Andrea Stember. I must thank my pastor Brian Croft for securing arrangements for this book's existence and for vouching for my own competence to compose it. Special thanks to Dr. Joanna Lile, Scott and Jay Wells, Dan McGill, Bryce Butler, Cindy Weber, and Jesse Eubanks for proofreading chapter drafts. My personal appreciation also extends to Dan Trabue and Jenilee Roddy for their research assistance.

Adam Garland Winters
May 31, 2016

1

THE PRODIGAL LIFE
OF STEVE P. HOLCOMBE

The most substantial testimony to the life of Steve P. Holcombe is available to us courtesy of his dear friend Gross Alexander (1852 – 1915), who wrote *Steve P. Holcombe, The Converted Gambler: His Life and Work*, originally published in 1888. Published only three years after the official establishment of the Union Gospel Mission, Alexander's biography provides us with Holcombe's testimony of how his faith in Jesus Christ revived his soul from "a gambler and doer of evil deeds" into "a preacher of the Gospel and a doer of all good," as Alexander himself wrote in the opening paragraph of the biography.[1] Having played a pivotal role in Holcombe's Christian conversion, perhaps no other man was more qualified to recount his life story.

The Reverend Alexander was a renaissance man in the Methodist Episcopal Church South, notable for service to congregations and in higher education. A pastor and a scholar, Alexander served as a chaplain (1885) and a professor of Greek and New Testament at Vanderbilt University from (1886 – 1902).[2] He pastored Methodist churches in Kentucky and Tennessee and spent his later years as the editor of the *Methodist Quarterly Review*. In addition to his biography on Holcombe, Alexander also authored works on Christian doctrine, education, and the history of the Methodist Church

South.[3] His personal connection to Holcombe owed to the fact that he held the distinction of being his first pastor and played a direct role in the conversion of the notorious gambler.

HOLCOMBE'S FORMATIVE YEARS

The man who would one day come to be known publically as Louisville's "converted gambler" was born in Shippingport, Kentucky on August 25, 1835.[4] A triangular shaped peninsula located adjacent to Louisville's Portland neighborhood among the Falls of Ohio River, Shippingport became a popular loading stop for merchant ships in the early nineteenth century, hence earning the community its name. By the time Gross Alexander published his biography on Holcombe in 1888, the river port had degraded into a shell of its former glory; his description of the town was unflattering:

> "In the very midst of all this profusion of beauty and all this hum and buzz and rush of commercial and social life, lies the dingy, sleepy old town of Shippingsport with its three hundred or four hundred people, all unheeded and unheeding, uncared for and uncaring. There are five or six fairly good houses, and all the rest are poor. There is a good brick school-house, built and kept up by the city of Louisville, of which, since 1842, Shippingsport is an incorporated port."[5]

Alexander also recorded his impression of the spiritual poverty of Shippingport:

> "There is one dilapidated, sad looking, little old brick church, which seldom suffers any sort of disturbance. . . . There are, at this time, some excellent people in Shippingsport, who faithfully maintain spiritual life and good moral

character amid surrounding apathy and immorality. 'For except the Lord had left unto them a very small remnant, they should have been as Sodom, and they should have been like unto Gomorrah.' "[6]

Alexander attributed the economic downturn of the town to the completion of the Louisville canal in 1830, noting that "when the canal was finished, the days of Shippingsport's prosperity were numbered.... The better classes lost no time in removing to other places, and only the poorer and rougher classes remained."[7] The canal allowed steamboats a convenient bypass to the peninsula in low water seasons which had served as a navigational hub and bustling commercial port since the Lewis and Clark Expedition.[8] The great steamboats and their passengers no longer bestowed their wealth on the small local community. Holcombe's parents moved to Shippingport in the year of his birth, but by 1835 the once prominent town had deteriorated into a shell of its former prosperity.

The dilapidated social structure of Shippingport offered a significant array of temptations for a young boy lacking strong parental oversight. Within the Holcombe household, there was a notable scarcity of moral and spiritual guidance that might have deterred young Steve from getting comfortable in habitual sins. Alexander's biography of Holcombe paints a tragic picture of how the failures of the parents impoverish their progeny:

> "It is hard enough for a boy to keep from doing wrong and to do right always, even when he has inherited a good disposition, enjoyed good advantages and had the best of training. But our little friend, Steve Holcombe, poor fellow, inherited from his father an appetite for drink and from his mother a savage temper. To balance these, he had none of the safeguards of a careful, moral or religious education,

and none of those sweet and helpful home associations which follow a man through life and hold him back from wrong doing."[9]

The paternal head of the Holcombe home was a poor model of manhood. As Steve recounted to Alexander:

> "My poor father had gotten to be a confirmed drunkard before I was born, and after he had settled at Shippingsport, my mother would not let him stay about the house, so that most of his time was spent in lying around bar-rooms or out on the commons, where he usually slept all times of the year."[10]

Steve's father died at the age of only thirty-three, leaving the young Holcombe fatherless at the age of eleven. While his father left him an example of wanton living, his mother left him an example of strong will and compassion for the poor:

> "When aroused ... she was as fierce as a tigress and fearless of God, man, or devil, although she was a woman of quick sympathy and impulsive kindheartedness toward those who were in distress, and would go further to help such than almost any one I have ever known."[11]

Steve Holcombe's youthful rebellion certainly cannot be attributed to this mother's lack of efforts to instill discipline in the lad:

> "Though my father ... never whipped me but once in my life, and that slightly, my mother has whipped me hundreds of times, I suppose, and with as great severity as frequency. She has, at times, almost beaten me to death. She would

use a switch, a cane, a broom-stick, or a club, whichever happened to be at hand when she became provoked. She whipped me oftener for going swimming than for anything else, I believe. If I told her a lie about it she would whip me, and if I told her the truth, she would whip me."[12]

His mother's tough love, while surely well-intentioned, was not sufficient to drive the future preacher to repentance and faith. On the other hand, his mother's remarkable displays of hospitality to strangers almost certainly helped sow the seeds of benevolence which God would later mold into the foundations for his rescue ministry work. Even at a young age, Holcombe showed evidence that this aspect of his mother's character was forming a sympathetic ethic for his fellow man. He recalled an incident when he, between the ages of five and six years old, discovered a stranger in an old shed who had been beaten and left for dead after a scrimmage in a Shippingport tavern; the young boy brought the stranger food every day for nearly two weeks.[13]

LOVE OF SIN, TORTURED CONSCIENCE

Though exercising his capacity for compassion upon the down-trodden, young Holcombe was also no stranger to boyhood mischief. From his childhood peers, he learned the thrill of petty theft even from his own kin. Around the age of seven, he dishonored his mother's instructions to sell cakes, pies, and fruits to passing steamboat passengers to earn the family extra income by squandering away the received money through gambling with his boyhood friends. Such instances earned him many of his mother's frequent and severe beatings. Well before his teenage years, Holcombe's gambling addictions had graduated into barroom card games with men.[14] As a ten-year-old with especially light colored hair, he gained the inglorious nickname "Little White-headed Pirate" due to his reputation of paddling around the Ohio Falls in a skiff rummaging for trinkets he might use as gambling fodder.[15]

Of these youthful follies, Holcombe later wrote that his entire purpose was to fashion his meager life into that of a professional gambler:

> "I learned to play cards at about the age of seven; and gambled for money at ten. In my youthful experience as a gambler I was a failure, so far as gains were concerned, as I almost invariably lost. But, notwithstanding my constant losses and my mother's terrible beatings, a gambler I would be. In these early days gamblers were called 'black-legs,' and I thought this a literal description of them. But notwithstanding this stigma, the height of my ambition was to be a gambler. And I succeeded admirably."[16]

Having settled upon his life's ambition, Holcombe had very little interest in wasting time with anything else. When Shipping-port became an official extension of the city of Louisville in 1842, a local school for children opened. Holcombe's childhood education was brief, estimated at three months, but it proved sufficient time for him to meet a young classmate named Mary Elizabeth Evans, who would eventually become his wife for more than fifty years and the moral anchor that kept him from ultimate self-ruin in the pursuit of his own insatiable appetites. Young Miss Evans developed an immediate affection for the little white-headed pirate.

Alexander summarized their childhood affection with almost poetic eloquence:

> "She did not know that she was in love with a boy who was to become one of the worst of men in all forms of wickedness, and as little did she know that she was in love

with a boy who was to become one of the best of men in all forms of goodness and usefulness. Nor did he foresee that he was forming an attachment then and there for one who was to love him devotedly and serve him patiently through all phases of infidelity and wickedness, and through years of almost unexampled trials and sufferings, who was to cling to him amid numberless perils and scandals, who was to train and restrain his children so as to lead them in ways of purity and goodness in spite of the father's bad example, who was to endure for his sake forms of ill treatment that have killed many a woman and who was in long distant years to be his most patient encourager and helper in a singularly blessed and successful work for God and the most abandoned and hopeless class of sinful men, and to develop, amid all and in spite of all and by means of all, one of the truest and strongest and most devoted of female characters."[17]

Only eleven years of age, Holcombe ran away from his mother's home and secured employment as a kitchen servant upon a Tennessee River steamboat, an experience which hardened his survival skills in society's underbelly. After experiencing some physical abuse from the boat's crew, he returned home with a growing resolve for his own self-sufficiency in the world. Over the next three years, Alexander estimated that Holcombe embarked on "four or five long steamboat runs" while spending as much time as could be spared in gambling.[18]

At the age of fourteen, Holcombe expanded his territory northward along the Mississippi River including cities like St. Louis, Missouri. On the steamboats, he witnessed a plethora of professional gamblers, decked out in fine attire, swindle money from wealthy passengers. The impression of a gambler so favorably fixed upon his mind, there was no deterring Holcombe for the pursuit of life as a high roller on the rivers.

Around this pivotal time in his early development, the Christian gospel confronted Holcombe and challenged his sense of self. He attended a revival in Shippingport which left a profound impression upon him to want to be a Christian, though he vainly sought to fashion himself into one through self-determination. Alexander noted that "for a week or ten days he succeeded in overcoming evil impulses, and in living right, but he was led away by evil companions."[19] Although young Holcombe tried on multiple occasions to cultivate such ideals of ascetic discipline, he ultimately returned to his vices, yielding to the temptations offered upon the steamboats.

The biblical verse of 2 Peter 2:22—which likens morally back-slidden false professors to dogs that return to their own vomit—might well be applied to this stage of Holcombe's life. A night of carousing with friends resulted in Holcombe joining his foolish companions in the physical abuse of a thirsty Shippingport beggar. They left the man for dead. The next day, Holcombe learned that the man had died overnight, and his conscience testified against him to such a degree that he might have fled to Indiana for sanctuary if not for the cause of death being determined as "death from exposure to the sun."[20] To whatever degree the young boys might have been responsible for the beggar's death, Holcombe understood himself to be guilty. Holcombe abandoned his experiment with Christianity and moral self-improvement. Sadly, this would not be the only blood he would have on his conscience.

The Allure of Sin and the Pull of True Love

His next stint on a steamboat to St. Louis almost resulted in another fatal encounter. A contentious exchange with a deckhand enticed Holcombe to threaten the man with a meat-cleaver. The intervention of the ship's cook ultimately diffused the situation. Similar incidents characterized his other steamboat expeditions throughout his adolescence; one incident involved chasing a man with an ice pick and another saw him actually strike a sleeping deckhand on the head with a cord-stick he brandished aboard the vessel.[21] Reflecting back upon this dark point in his life, Holcombe later confessed to his pastor and biographer, "I can not understand how a man could do so cruel a thing, but *then* I felt I must have revenge some way, and *I could not keep from it.*"[22]

Traveling along the banks of the Mississippi River, Holcombe cultivated his gambling habits in the seedy establishments found in Kansas City, St. Louis, New Orleans, and Galveston, Texas. The gambling he witnessed at stops along the Mississippi River involved considerably higher stakes than he had ever before witnessed. Large sums of money changed hands at a rapid pace, and this had an intoxicating effect upon Holcombe, who immersed himself further into the lifestyle.[23]

Having physically matured into early adulthood, Holcombe's failures in gambling had left him penniless. Struggling under the additional burdens of years of guilt, loneliness, and fear of men, Holcombe sought to better himself through pursuing the love of his childhood friend Mary Evans, so he returned to her at Shippingport. The Evans household did not permit Holcombe to visit their abode, but he managed to see Mary in other social opportunities around the small community. Despite her parents' disapproval and much counsel from friends to decline his advances, Mary's affections for him endured. Strikingly, even Holcombe's own mother warned Mary to no avail that "she was going to marry the very devil."[24]

The couple married in 1855, after Holcombe arranged to meet her at a friend's house and proposed an immediate elopement.[25] The boldness initially unnerved Miss Evans, but her suitor persisted with urgency, even daring to offer the ultimatum, "It must be tonight or never."[26] Neither the Evans household nor Holcombe's mother consented to the union, but they were nevertheless wed at the house of Mrs. Holcombe. Though Holcombe's degenerate reputation had been well established around the Shippingport community, his marriage gave him renewed vigor to better himself into a respectable provider for his family.

Holcombe initially abandoned his riverboat escapades and aspired to refashion himself as a fisherman. Alexander noted in the biography that the newly married couple did join a church within the first three months of their marriage, despite neither of the Holcombes identifying as Christian. Alexander withheld the name of the specific church fellowship, perhaps so as not to pass judgment upon the soul-care of the congregation or its ministers. The Holcombes interest in church membership came out of a sense of social duty and a desire towards moral improvement. Alexander's assessment of this phenomenon reveals his own displeasure with the faithfulness of the congregation's soul care:

> "If [the Holcombes] had had some one, wise and patient and faithful, to teach them and advise them and sympathize with them at this time of awakening and of honest endeavor after a spiritual life, they would probably have gone on happily and helpfully together in it. But alas! As is true in so many, many cases to-day, nobody understood or seemed to understand them, nobody tried or cared to understand them; nobody cared for their souls. It was taken for granted, then as now, that when people are gotten into the church, nothing special is to be done for them any further, though, in fact, the most difficult and delicate part of training a soul and developing Chris-

tian character comes after conversion and after joining the church."[27]

Of Holcombe's spiritual condition, Alexander wrote:

"In such a nature as his, especially, no mere form of religion and no external bond of union with the church was sufficient. The strength of his will, the tenacity of his old habits, the intensity of his nature and the violence of his passions were such that only an extraordinary power would suffice to bring him under control."[28]

Holcombe's temporary zeal for moral uprightness soon dissipated and his lacking family values pained his bride—still haunted by her mother-in-law's prior warning about her marriage to "the very devil." In perhaps the most somber paragraph of his entire biography on Holcombe, Alexander noted that:

"And Mr. Holcombe found out, too, that his wife, good as she was, could not make him good. Some men there are so hungry-hearted and so dependent that they can not endure life without the supreme and faithful and submissive affection of a wife, but who know not how to appreciate or treat a wife and soon lose that consideration and love for her which are her due. Then marriage becomes tyranny on the one side and slavery on the other."[29]

As for Mary, she invested herself in her children's upbringing almost single-handedly, even seeking to teach them a sense of Christian morality despite her own absence of a profession of faith. After the birth of the Holcombes' first child, she ceased from personally practicing many of the worldly amusements which had previously pleased her husband. She would bear her husband both boys and girls throughout their union, and she tried her best to conceal most of his vices from them to the best of her ability.[30]

BACK IN THE GAME, BUT DEEPER IN DEBT

Holcombe returned to gambling as a hobby and side pursuit of his various attempts at business. In 1860, he relocated his family to Nashville, Tennessee to open a business dealership for importing fish and oysters from Louisville. By this point, the couple had propagated two children, though the second-born child perished prematurely soon before the move. This tragedy compounded the sorrow of Mary Holcombe as she watched her husband return to his old vices and spend his nights gambling the family income among his business partners. The exotic culinary offerings of the Nashville business proved considerably profitable until the outbreak of the Civil War squeezed away its supply route to Louisville.[31]

Holcombe struggled to find alternative means of income and even marched with Kentucky soldiers from Clarksville, Tennessee to Bowling Green, Kentucky, where he opened a grocery store that he eventually exchanged for a monetary claim on the Confederate government. He was able to collect on the claim and reunite with his family in Nashville. Holcombe suffered with severe bouts of sickness during the Civil War years as he sought to secure financial support for his family, but his passion for gambling took a new twist when his poker playing partners introduced him to the game of faro.

Entranced by the ease by which he was able to learn the card game's rules, Holcombe immediately sunk hundreds of dollars into it. All his poker nights entertaining the local businessmen of Nashville gave him the confidence to return to Louisville to open a gambling house dedicated to faro gaming. At this point,

Holcombe had no interest in making a living through any other means than professional gambling. Looking back upon this point in his life from the hindsight of almost forty years, Holcombe wrote:

> "I gave up all attempts at any other business or occupation, and begun my career as a professional gambler. I followed this life for seventeen years, and oh, what years! It frightens me now to recall them. There is nothing in them pleasant for me to remember, they were one constant experience of sin and pain."[32]

Predictably, Holcombe went broke again, but that was only the beginning of one of the darkest periods of his unrepentant life. In Shippingport, out of a sense of moral duty, he confronted a young man named Martin Mohler who had become intimately involved with Holcombe's half-sister, deceiving her with a false intent towards marriage. Holcombe brought a pistol with him to convince Mohler to make good on his vain proposal. The man's crass retort infuriated Holcombe, who rashly pulled the trigger and felled him.[33]

Holcombe's great crime immediately filled him with pity for the man whom he had shot. His own account of the night is a heart-wrenching scene:

> "When he fell he asked me to raise him up. Putting my arm under his neck, I did so, and held him until a doctor was called. I was now touched with pity for the man, and would have done anything in my power for him, but all my pity and repentance could not bring him back to life. I turned him over to a doctor, went into a bar-room and washed the blood from my hands, but I could not wash the blood from my conscience."[34]

Mohler died, and Holcombe was arrested and taken to jail. Surprisingly, the jury acquitted him at his trial, but no court's decision could alleviate Holcombe's deepening sense of internal guilt, as he noted:

> "No human sentence or approval of public opinion can quiet a guilty human conscience when awakened by the God whose soul prerogative of executing justice is guarded by His own solemn and awful words: 'Vengeance is mine. I will repay, saith the Lord.' "[35]

Holcombe cited this event as a defining moment which drew him down deeper into depraved living to distract him from his guilty conscience:

> "When the conscience is pressed with a great sense of guilt, it seeks relief by the way of contrition and repentance, or by a deeper plunge into sin and guilt, as if the antidote to a dose of poison were a larger dose of poison. There is no middle ground unless it be insanity, nor did I find any middle ground. I did not allow myself to think of the killing of the man; and I had to keep very busy in a career of sin, to keep from thinking about it."[36]

He continued to pursue his faro gaming business across Louisville and Nashville, but by 1869 he had settled his family in Augusta, Georgia. At this point in the marriage, the Holcombe household had become a depressingly bleak place for Mary and her four children as her husband's frequent drunkenness contributed to harsh and unrestrained outbursts of his temper. His drunken fits of rage sometimes involved the destruction of home furniture, the overturning of dining tables already set with food, the shattering of kitchenware, and the verbal berating of the only woman who had ever showed him genuine affection. Mary simply endured his deplorable conduct by sitting in silence, "not in fear, but in grief; for she knew as little of fear as he."[37]

Mary later recalled:

"Much of my time was spent in walking the floor and grieving. Often in my loneliness and sorrow my lips would cry out, 'How can I endure this life any longer?' I had not then become a Christian and did not know what I do now about taking troubles and burdens to God. And yet I believe that it was God who comforted my heart more than once when my sorrow was more than I could bear. I cried to Him without knowing Him. All these years I tried to raise my children right, and I taught them to respect their father. I hid his sins from them when I could, and when I could not, I always excused him to them the best I could."[38]

The Holcombes relocated from Augusta to Atlanta, with Steve making various excursions chasing gambling opportunities and hastily-gotten gain. After going bankrupt betting on a race in Nashville, he entered into an uneasy partnership with a man named Buchanan to work their tricks around the South in tandem. This southern excursion took Holcombe to major urban environments across Georgia, Louisiana, Texas, Florida and even Cuba. One morning in Shreveport, Louisiana led to a gunpoint confrontation between Holcombe and Buchanan in which the former once again pulled the trigger with intent to harm, but this time the gun misfired and the two men had a chance to settle their dispute peaceably. After they left the bar-room, a friend of Holcombe's shot another acquaintance to death. To quote Holcombe's somber estimation: "And such is the life of the gambler."[39]

Perhaps as an early foretaste of God's grace in his life, Holcombe was again spared the experience of shooting another man in Beaufort, South Carolina after a bar fight followed a gambling dispute. His fellow pugilist's aggression finally subsided once Holcombe drew his pistol and threatened to shoot. Sensing that staying in that town would inevitably lead to the death of himself or the other man, Holcombe returned home.

In the 1870s, the Holcombes settled in Louisville once again in the interest of establishing a faro business. This time around, Holcombe made efforts to save enough money to invest in housing in the city's west end. Alexander insightfully noted in the biography that such actions indicated an early tempering of Holcombe's wandering spirit and a precursor of the great spiritual renewal that he was soon to experience:

> "Poor man! He had wandered *nearly* enough. He had almost found that rest can not be found, at least in the way that he was seeking it, and the time was approaching when he would be *prepared* to hear of another sort and source of rest. Until he be prepared, it would be vain to send him the message. To give the truth in some people today would be to cast pearls before swine, to give it to them tomorrow may be re-clothing banished princes with due tokens of welcome and royalty. To have told Steve Holcombe of Christ yet awhile would probably have excited his wonder and disgust; to tell him a little later will be to welcome a long-lost, long-enslaved, and perishing child to his Father's house and to all the liberty of the sons of God."[40]

Holcombe's own assessment of his spiritual condition echoed his pastor's words:

"After wandering over almost the whole world, seeking rest for my weary heart, and finding it not, I returned to Louisville, the place of my birth, and the place where I committed the great crime that caused all my restlessness. . . . At this time thoughts of a better life came to me. And God was thinking too, and just like Him, He was thinking thoughts and kindness and love for the poor, wicked gambler; yea, He was more than thinking. He was getting things ready. Truth and God are always ready, but man is not always ready."[41]

Though thinking more responsibly toward the future, Holcombe continued to take gambling excursions across Kentucky and northern states such as Indiana, Michigan, Ohio, and New York. Ultimately, however, it was the city of Louisville that would cement itself as the home for the Holcombes in the fateful year of 1877. During that year, a series of events would wreak upheaval upon Holcombe's life, ultimately transforming him into a new man. The rascally reputation that had characterized him for nearly forty years would soon culminate in the remarkable story of "The Converted Gambler."

2

THE CONVERTED
GAMBLER AND THE
HOLCOMBE MISSION

William, affectionately called "Willie"—the eldest of the Holcombes' children at about seventeen-years-old—had seen his father
come home drunk and battered too many times to count. He had
developed a desperate heart to see his father break the habit of
intoxication. At an 1877 city meeting of the temperance movement,
the boy signed a card pledging never to drink liquor. When Willie
brought the card home to his father, Holcombe became so emo-
tionally moved by his son's concern for him that he too attended
a temperance meeting the following night. Previously, Willie had
begged his father to return home whenever he spotted him drinking in public. And with Mary by his side, Steve Holcombe finally
did his oldest boy proud by signing a temperance pledge that night.[1]

The child continued to lead his family in the way of godliness.
Willie made arrangements with Broadway Baptist Church—one
of the city's most revered Baptist congregations that would become
home to many of Louisville's great Baptist luminaries such as James
Petigru Boyce of The Southern Baptist Theological Seminary—to
baptize him, and he invited his parents to attend. Holcombe's
affections were stirred by witnessing his son immersed under the
baptismal waters, even vowing to his wife that "I will never play
another card."[2] Mary cried for joy at such a bold promise, but most

31

of Holcombe's peers doubted the vow would hold true. For the rest of the year, Holcombe held himself to his promise, and sought once again to enter into the business of produce sales. His finances were tied up with the houses he owned in the Portland neighborhood, and he rented out the very home in which he lived in hopes of relocating closer to the heart of the city's commerce district.

LIFE-CHANGING ENCOUNTER

Holcombe's business operated out of Main Street, and on a life-changing day in October of 1877, a gentleman entered his store in order to inquire about renting the Portland house. That man was Gross Alexander, a young minister newly called to a Methodist church in the Portland neighborhood. "That settles it then, sir," Holcombe responded, "I am a notorious gambler, and of course, you would not want to live in a house of mine."[3] Alexander simply laid his hand upon Holcombe's shoulder and said, "On no, my brother; I do not object to living in your house; and who knows but that this interview will result in good to us both, in more ways than one?"[4] And the Methodist minister promptly invited the former gambler to come to his church.

Holcombe accepted the invitation the following Sunday, intrigued to have "a good man" call him "brother" for the first time in his life.[5] Holcombe approached Alexander after the service to inquire about joining the church, and Alexander welcomed him. Holcombe recounted his experience in Alexander's Methodist church to be characterized by a far greater outpouring of soul care than his previous stint with church membership following his marriage:

> "From the day I joined the church ... that minister seemed to understand me better than I understood myself. He seemed to know and did tell me my own secrets. He led

me into an understanding of myself and my situation. I saw now what had been the cause of my restlessness, my wanderings, my weariness and my woe. I saw what it was I needed, and I prayed as earnestly as I knew how from that time. I attended all the services—preaching, Sunday-school, prayer-meeting, class meeting in any and all kinds of weather, walking frequently all the way from Second street to Portland, a distance of three miles, because I was making too little to allow me to ride on the street-cars."[6]

Despite his newfound kinship with Rev. Alexander and the Portland Methodist fellowship, Holcombe's spiritual awakening had not yet culminated in a personal knowledge with Jesus Christ. That encounter soon occurred once Holcombe saw his life of sin as a burden to be cast off at the foot of the cross of Christ:

"I found something was yet wanting. I began to see that I could not make any advance in goodness and happiness so long as I was burdened with the unforgiven guilt of forty years of sin and crime. It grew worse and heavier until I felt I must have relief, if relief could be had. One day I went in the back office of my business house, after the others had all gone home, and shut myself up and determined to stay there and pray until I should find relief. The room was dark, and I had prayed, I know not how long, when such a great sense of relief and gladness and joy came to me as if a light had flooded the room, and the only words I could utter or think of were these three: 'Jesus of Nazareth.' It seemed to me they were the sweetest words I had ever heard. Never till then, did the feeling of blood guiltiness leave me. It was only the blood of Christ that could wash from my conscience the blood of my fellowman."[7]

Steve Holcombe—the wanderer, the pugnacious bar room brawler, the ungrateful husband, the absent father, the gambler, and the murderer—finally knew repentance, faith, and forgiveness in Christ. This experience was no fleeting emotional elation without true root in the heart, as Holcombe himself confessed regarding that night of epiphany in his business office:

> "While in that room, shut out from the whole world, alone with God, I had a sight of my own heart, and oh, how black it was, made so by the blood I had shed fourteen years before. I believed in Jesus, and ever since that day, I too can sing with other blood-washed sinners: 'Oh, precious is the flow, No other fount I know, Nothing but the blood of Jesus.' "[8]

Rev. Alexander did not leave the newly converted Holcombe without discipleship to mature him in his sanctification. Holcombe, though being nearly two decades their senior, received true Christian hospitality from both the minister and his wife. For nearly two years, this new Christian fellowship filled his life richly to such a degree that he put to death his desires for his old vices which had previously obsessed him:

> "Seeing the great necessity of giving me much attention and making me feel at home in his presence and in the presence of his wife he spent much time in my company, and with loving patience bore with my ignorance, dullness and slowness. In this way, I became so much attached to him that I had no need or desire for my old associations. He led me along till I was entirely weaned from all desire for my old sinful life and habits. I think he gave me this close attention for about two years when he felt

it was best for me to lean more upon God and less upon him."[9]

Holcombe began to grow into the spiritual leader of his own household. To his own great joy, his family—Mary, Willie, and his two daughters Mayme and Irene—joined the Portland Methodist church that Alexander pastored. In this way, the ties that bound his heart to Christ also translated into a greater intimacy with his immediate family. With the support of his family circle, Holcombe aspired to share the good news of salvation in Jesus with all men currently engaged in the fruitless lifestyle that had formerly characterized his own existence. His post-conversion life became one which sought to imitate the gracious hospitality shown to him by the Alexander household, even at the sacrificial cost of personal comforts:

"From the time of his conversion, he had a deep and brotherly sympathy for all who were without the knowledge and joy he had come into the possession of, but he felt a special interest in the salvation of the wretched and the outcast, and the men of his own class and former occupation who were as ignorant as he was of these higher things and as shut out from opportunities of knowing them. So that from the very beginning of his Christian life he undertook to help others, and when they were in need, not stopping to think of any other way, he took them to his own house. This, with the support of his own family, increased the cost of his living to such an extent that he was soon surprised and pained to find that he could not carry on his business. He had taken to his home, also, the father of his wife, whom he cared for till his death. And in a short time he was so pressed for means that he had to mortgage his property for money to go into another kind of business."[10]

FAITH TESTED

Holcombe's newfound faith promptly underwent a purity testing; within two years of his conversion, his business went bankrupt, and he was forced to sell his property without any sizeable return in his investment. Instead of returning to his old gambling habits in his desperation to feed his family, he decided to seek out financial opportunities in Colorado, a popular region for mountain prospecting if one had the means to finance an expedition. This decision caused the Rev. Alexander great distress, as he feared such a drastic excursion might prove too many temptations for Holcombe to resist. Ultimately, Holcombe convinced his pastor that no alternative financial option existed, so Alexander committed his friend to God and gifted him with sixty-one dollars he had saved in the bank from before his marriage, saying "if that will pay your way out, you can have it. Christ has called for his own."[11] Holcombe set aside some of the money for his family as he left them in desperate hopes of finding firm financial footing in the West.

Temptation wasted no time finding Holcombe in Denver. He encountered an old gambling comrade from his Atlanta residence named John Chisholm who was operating a faro gaming establishment. Chisholm—who was facing his own financial troubles at the time and may have been on the run from Georgia for murder— invited Holcombe to join him as a partner in his enterprise, promising him good interest on a potential investment. Holcombe simply replied to his old friend, "but I am a Christian now, and cannot deal faro." Chisholm protested, "I know you were a Christian in Louisville, but you are a long ways from there." Decisively, Holcombe stated, "Yes, but a true Christian is a Christian everywhere."[12]

After exchanging pleasantries, Holcombe took leave of Chisholm and left Denver for Silver Cliff. Penniless upon his arrival, Holcombe was too impoverished to even pay his stage-driver. His dishonorable state left him weeping and fearful of the future. Like Denver, Silver Cliff offered a plethora of temptations toward gambling, courtesy of two of his old acquaintances. Instead of casting his lot with the gamblers, he found humble employment as a dining-room waiter at the Carbonate hotel in which he spent his first night in town. His salary included twenty-five dollars a month and board—an income which was a far cry from his more successful days in business and gambling, but one for which he was thankful to God for the provision.

By May of 1879, Holcombe had saved enough money from hotel table waiting to invest in a mountain prospecting outfit, which included a diminutive donkey, picking equipment, and about a half month's worth of provisions. He partnered with a Wisconsin man named J. E. White to seek fortune in the mountains and kept a diary of their adventure from May 27 until June 18.[13] The prospecting was unfruitful, the weather was cold and snowy, and the overall experience was greatly taxing upon Holcombe's health and soul. He suffered not only physical discomforts but also the emotional pain of being so far away from his family in Louisville. His great spiritual sustainment came from daily chapter readings from the book of Romans, which gave his soul peace as he lay down to sleep every night.

After giving up on the mountain picking, the men returned to Silver Creek and sold their donkey. The prospecting expedition having failed, Holcombe resolved to return home using whatever means available. Accompanied by a friend from Silver Creek, his journey was long and hard, as he walked on foot for miles and bargained his personal belongings to hitchhike, eat, and board for nights whenever possible. For a man who only owned one pair of pants and socks, this was a truly uncomfortable burden to endure.[14] During this journey home, Holcombe confessed to learning a valuable lesson about showing charity to strangers.[15]

After returning to Denver, he found charitable hospitality from another old friend named Frank Jones, who offered Holcombe space in his room. Holcombe found work in a brick-yard for three weeks until he found himself physically exhausted and broke once again. In his desperation, he was tempted to ask for help from the local Young Men's Christian Association, but he feared they would have no sympathy upon him and, furthermore, his pride prevented him from asking favors of others, even like-minded Christians. At this time, his thoughts drifted to memories of lodging in luxurious hotels, wearing fine clothes, and eating expensive meals with money earned through sin and vice.[16]

In this dark moment, Holcombe preached to himself the words of Job 13:15: "Yea, and though He slay me, yet will I trust in Him."[17] He realized that he must return immediately to Louisville, and his friend Jones was charitable enough to buy him a ticket to Kansas City, Missouri. From Kansas City, Holcombe received further compassion from the temperance lecturer Francis Murphy, who paid the necessary expenses for Holcombe's return to Louisville.

Alexander remarked that this Colorado excursion served to mature the faith of Holcombe:

> "Without the experiences and lessons of this Colorado trip, Mr. Holcombe could not have been the efficient man he is to-day. That season of loneliness and self-searching and severe testing and humiliation was to him, though a painful, yet a helpful, and perhaps necessary, stage in his Christian life. . . . Moreover, if he was to serve efficiently the poor and the tempted, he needed to become acquainted

with their condition, their sorrows, their conflicts, by pass-ing through them himself."[18]

MISSIONARY IN LOUISVILLE

He discovered that his family in Louisville had struggled mightily during his western excursion. In Steve's absence, Mary Holcombe could not pay her rent and had to remove from her house while striving to be the sole financial supporter of the family through sewing work. For six weeks more, Steve sought in vain for adequate work while Mary sewed to keep the household from starving.

Economic relief came in the form of Holcombe's friend Major Ed Hughes, Chief of the Fire Department of Louisville, who hired him for a subordinate job in the department's engine house on Portland Avenue at a meager salary of $1.50 per day, not quite enough to support a family but with Mary supplementing the income by selling sewn coats, they were able to persevere. Work in the engine house over the next two years proved taxing on Hol-combe, and his schedule kept him busy working night and day, even on Sunday. Holcombe later reflected upon this time in his life as an important means of teaching him patience, which better prepared him for his mission work.[19]

As physically taxing as the work in the engine house could be, the aspect which troubled him most was how little time he had for doing gospel ministry:

> "The close and slavish confinement, the necessity of being always at my place, both of nights and Sundays, and the consequent lack of opportunity to do anything for the cause of my Master, made it almost intolerable for me, and several times I made up my mind I would give up the place, even though I had nothing else to fall back on for a living for myself and family. . . . I determined I must do something

for my Lord and for the men of my acquaintance and
former occupation who would not, I knew, go inside
of a church."[20]

Even during these two hard years of fire engine cleaning, Holcombe sought to use what little free time he had to organize
religious services around Louisville and Shippingport focused upon
the poor, "with the hope of helping and blessing them."[21] Sometimes, Holcombe even decided to withdraw from the engine house
for ministry, home duties, and church attendance, but this temporary freedom required him to hire a substitute in his place at his
own expense. He would occasionally invite struggling men into his
own home in hopes of edifying them with the gospel, although he
later regretting putting the additional burden of such charity upon
his family. On that matter, Alexander wrote that "such was his
insatiable longing to help and bless others, he let his zeal, perhaps,
go beyond his prudence in that single particular."[22]

One frightful night illustrated this point vividly: one of Holcombe's downtrodden house guests suffered an attack of
deliriousness, causing him to hear violent voices in his head ordered
him to murder the Holcombe family. The man, described as
"demonized," entered the Holcombes' master bedroom brandish-
ing a razor. Mary's shrieks awoke Steve, who was able to restrain
the man's advances before he was able to slaughter the couple in
their bed. After which point, Holcombe sat up to monitor the
houseguest who continued to converse with the devilish voices
torturing his mind. Over the course of the following day, Holcombe
did his best to keep close to this besieged man and eventually called
him a physician when he feared himself being choked to death by
the spirit of a deceased friend.[23]

Holcombe's unceasing charity evidenced toward the poor and
troubled men of Louisville left a deep impression upon the Rev.

Alexander of the mighty work of grace God was doing in the heart of Louisville's famous converted gambler. Alexander sensed that if any opportunity should arise by which his church could advance the cause of the gospel in the city, Holcombe would be the right man to lead such an effort. Thus, he continued to visit regularly with Holcombe during his engine house work so that he might teach and encourage his spiritual brother in the event such an opportunity should arise. Although Holcombe struggled with book reading, he eventually became an adept student and careful reader of text.[24] Holcombe's presence in the engine house also had the apparent effect of restraining some of the vices of the department's other employees, who greatly respected the consistency of his Christian profession and life to such a degree that they guarded their tongues from obscene and profane language.[25]

THE METHODIST MISSION

By 1881, Holcombe greatly desired to move beyond his menial engine house labors into sustained ministerial work directed toward Louisville's lowest social classes. He even made arrangements to rent a room in the center of the city to hold religious services. Before he could even finalize that effort, the Methodist ministers of Louisville met together with respect to the remarkable conversion story of Steve Holcombe. There was interest among those Methodist ministers to employ the unique talents and passion of Holcombe in an official denominational capacity, but they did not organize any official plan. James C. Morris, the pastor of the Methodist church on Walnut Street, took the initiative in establishing a gospel mission in the central part of the city supported directly by his particular congregation.[26] He paid Holcombe a personal visit at the engine house to offer him the responsibility of direct charge over the Mission with an assured salary of $900 a year, a sum sufficient to support his family.[27]

Morris had never met Holcombe prior to this meeting in the engine house, but he had become well aware of his reputation:

"In the year 1881 ... I heard of Steve Holcombe, the converted gambler, of his respectable career; of his remarkable conversion, and of his unusual devotion and zeal in the cause of religion. I heard also of his efforts in the line of Christian work and of his desire for better opportunities. I mentioned his case to the Official Board of the Walnut-Street church, and suggested that he might be usefully employed by our churches in the city in doing missionary work. The matter was kindly received, but the suggestion took no practical shape. As I walked home from the meeting one of the stewards said to me: 'Why could not we, of the Walnut-street church, employ Brother Holcombe ourselves?' This question put me on the course of thought about the work we might be able to do, and at the next meeting of the Board I made the suggestion that we organize some work of the kind and employ Brother Holcombe to take charge of it. They unanimously accepted the suggestion and directed me to investigate the case. If anything could be done, they were ready to enter upon the work and support it."[28]

In an August 14, 1888 letter to Alexander, Morris recalled his first encounter with Holcombe in the fire engine house:

"It took but a moment to introduce myself and in a short time we were upstairs, talking about religion and work for Christ. He told me how his heart was drawn out in solicitude for the classes who never attended church—the gamblers, drunkards, and the like. It was easy to see that the movement contemplated was of God. We talked and rejoiced together; we knelt down and prayed together for God's guidance in all our plans and undertakings. I then told him how I came to call on him, and laid before him our plan. His eyes filled with tears—tears of joy—at the thought of having an opportunity to do the work that was on his heart."[29]

The location of the Walnut Street Methodist church's new Mission was a vacant store in the Tyler Block, on Jefferson Street between Third Street and Fourth Street, which Morris and Holcombe were able to operate free of rent expenses thanks to the generosity of its owner, Isaac Tyler.[30] This Mission, which would soon come to be synonymous with Holcombe, was ironically situated within two blocks of the faro gambling houses with he had once owned. Now, Holcombe was charged with ministry to the downtrodden and the preaching of the gospel. Within four years of having been converted from a life of bondage to vice and violence, the divine work of transformation in his soul was now plain for all to witness.

Alexander described Holcombe's preaching style in the Mission's early days, along with the public reaction:

"It was a phenomenon. . . . The people came to see and hear. They found it was no mushroom fanatic, but a man who for forty years was a leader in wickedness and for four years had been almost a pattern of righteousness. He spoke no hot words of excitement, but narrated facts with truth and soberness. Many of his old time friends, the gamblers, their timidity overcome by their curiosity, joined the crowd and heard the man. Poor drunkards, too far gone for timidity or curiosity, dragged themselves to the place where the famous gambler was telling about his conversion and his new life. And the power of God was present to heal, and great grace was upon them all."[31]

Meetings initially occurred three nights a week, but with such good attendance, public gatherings soon expanded to every day of the week. The order of services included singing, prayers, Scripture reading, shared testimonies, and concise but pointed sermons courtesy of Holcombe.[32] Morris detailed the nature of the meeting's visitors:

> "The services were advertised and men stationed at the door invited the passerby to come in. At the meetings all classes of men were represented. There were strong, wise, honorable, business men and there were tramps and drunkards with all the classes that lie between those two. No man was slighted. Many a man was brought in who was too drunk to sit alone in his seat. Men were there who had not slept in a bed for months. There were gamblers and drunkards and outcast men from every quarter of the city. The gathering looked more like that in the police courts of a great city on Monday morning than like a religious meeting. The workers did literally go out into the highways and into the lowways and compel them to come in. And marvelous things took place there."[33]

As for Holcombe himself, Morris recalled the early days of his Mission ministry as the picture of a man set free from all encumbrance, joyfully embracing the work God had given him:

> "Brother Holcombe was in his element. His soul was as free to the work as that of an Apostle. Daily he trod the streets inviting people to come, and daily, as they came, he

spoke words of deep feeling to them, urging them to be saved. No man ever had a more respectful hearing than he had. No man ever devoted himself more fully in the spirit of the Master to doing men good than did he. His devotion to the poor outcast who showed any willingness to listen or any wish to be saved was as marvelous as his own conversion. I never saw such in any other worker for Christ."[34]

The Mission's first three months of existence proved fruitful, but its success cannot be measured by statistics. In fact, no precise statistics were kept of converts or people served during the Mission's early years, much to the later regret of Rev. Morris:

"In the progress of the work, we often spoke of keeping a record of those who professed conversion there. I am sorry it was not done. Hardly a day passed without some case of exceptional interest. Men were saved who had been for years in the very lowest stages of dissipation and vagrancy. Not a few of those who were saved were men who had belonged to the very best social and business circles of the city. Many of them are bright and blessed lights in Christian circles to-day. Many homes were built up out of wrecks where only ashes and tears remained. Many scattered families were brought together after long separation. God only knows the results of that three months' work.... Mr. Holcombe had won thousands of friends, hundreds had been put in the way of a new life and the whole city was in sympathy with the work."[35]

EXPANSION OF THE MISSION
The public interest in Holcombe's Mission became so great that the Mission's supporters recognized a larger location would be

more suited to the expanding ministry. Thus, after three months in the store-room location, the Mission work moved about one block west into a room formerly used as a gambling house located at 436 Jefferson Street between Fourth and Fifth streets; Holcombe's own family resided above the Mission's assembly room in the same building.[36]

In 1882, the great revivalist Samuel Porter Jones held a meeting at the Walnut Street Methodist church and became aware of Holcombe's work with the Mission. Rev. Jones even held some services at the Mission, incorporating Holcombe and other Mission workers into a program of street preaching. Holcombe himself preached upon the courthouse steps and his message reaped many converts, and Jones's endorsement of Holcombe's life and work advanced the public reputation of the Mission. Jones later contributed an introduction to Holcombe's 1888 biography, describing him as "one man of whom it may be said: 'His conversation is in heaven.'"[37]

The work at this second manifestation of the "Gospel Mission"—the name by which Morris referred to it in his 1888 letter to Alexander—was considerably more ambitious than the first three months of its existence.[38] In addition to Holcombe's regular daily services, the Mission eventually established a Sunday School for children of non-church going parents. The first superintendent of the Sunday School was Colonel C. P. Atmore. A board of managers formed to provide administrative oversight to the Mission consisting of five men. The Walnut Street church supported the ministry through volunteer hymn-singing, supplying hymn books, and securing an organ.[39]

The Holcombe family, now living in the Mission's building, extended their Christian charity to all their guests. Men entered the Mission by the dozen to receive meals. Holcombe, whose own sense of compassion knew little limits, had to exercise discernment in identifying the earnest men in need from those who simply wanted to antagonize the work of the godly. His time among the wicked and the gamblers during his unconverted life had provided him with ample experience in dealing with insincere and dangerous men, and he feared no man. Alexander wrote:

> "Men would come into the meetings, sometimes, in a state of intoxication; sometimes lewd fellows of the baser sort would come in for the purpose of interrupting the service and still others for other purposes; but when Mr. Holcombe had put a few of them out, they saw that this man in getting religion had lost neither common sense nor courage, and that Steve Holcombe, the converted gambler, was not a man to be fooled with any more than Steve Holcombe, the unconverted gambler; so that all such interruptions soon ceased."[40]

Holcombe kept Alexander—who had by this time removed from Louisville—informed as to the Mission's progress through written correspondence, many of which Alexander later published in the biography:

November 6, 1883

"My Dear Brother:
Our meetings continue in interest. Last night the Holy Ghost was with us in great power. At the close of the talk, we invited backsliders to come forward and kneel. Six responded. Then we invited all others who wanted to become Christians to come forward and nine others responded, most of them the most hardened sinners in the city. I am sure nothing but the power of God could have

lifted them from their seats. Men who have fought each other actually embraced last night. Continue to pray for us."[41]

November 19, 1883
"Last night about two hundred persons were present, most of them non-churchgoers. About forty stood up for prayers. And oh, such good testimonies, no harangues but living testimonies as to what God can and will do for those who will let him.[42]"

In addition to the central meeting area at 436 Jefferson Street, Holcombe also held public services at other parts of the city, including preaching on the streets and the courthouse steps. The "Holcombe Mission," as it came to be known, gained a great reputation within the city of Louisville, and its work continued to expand. In April 1884, the Mission added an "Industrial School," Christian women taught young girls the art of sewing and furnished them all the necessary materials to create their own garments.[43] The superintendent of this school was Mrs. J. R. Clark, under whose oversight the school opened with six girls and three teachers. By the close of the Industrial School's first session in June, it had expanded to five teachers and twenty-two children, ranging in ages between five and eighteen.[44]

The Industrial School soon employed additional staff serving under Mrs. Clark, including Mrs. L. G. Herndon (Assistant Superintendent), Miss Ella Downing (Secretary), and Miss Ella Harding (Treasurer). The school continued its work in September with steadily increasing enrollment consisting of children "from all parts of the city, some of them from garrets and cellars."[45] The teachers in the school instructed the children not only in home economics so that they might better their physical comforts, but sewing lessons provided opportunity for the teachers to converse with the children regarding spiritual and religious topics.[46]

The Industrial School also expanded its scope to entail a class for boys. By 1886, the boys' class numbered sixty students between ages five and twelve. The boys were taught to sew on buttons and to mend clothing, belonging either to themselves or to their friends. The class of boys learned cooperation by teaming together to create a carpet for Holcombe's own office. Mrs. Clark identified the over-arching pedagogical goal for the boys' class to be training to "habits of industry, self-reliance, cleanliness, truthfulness, etc."[47] A typical Saturday morning service for the school would begin at 9:15 and consist of an hour and a half of sewing with hymn singing, responsive Bible readings, prayers, and Scripture repetition lessons preceding and following the instructional period.[48]

The Holcombe Mission continued to expand its ministries towards the city's poorer children in January of 1885 by opening a kindergarten school for children between the ages of three and five. The first kindergarten classes had an average attendance of twenty-four children and met on Saturday mornings as an alternative to the Industrial School's sewing sessions.[49] By February of the following year, the Holcombe Mission's board of directors recognized a sufficient increase of interest in the kindergarten ministry that a class was offered six days a week, and participation increased to sixty children with four women providing the training by June.[50]

With a rapidly expanding ministerial structure since its humble beginnings in 1881, the Holcombe Mission required a growing number of teachers and staff to meet all its growing needs. In addition to the direct support of the Walnut Street Methodist church, the Mission was blessed by many charitable and sympathetic friends who believed the Mission provided salt and light to urban Louisville. The increasingly public profile of

Holcombe himself was a great means towards raising funds and goodwill in the community. Furthermore, testimonies of the spiritual and moral transformations which Holcombe and his ministry had effected upon the drunkards and vagrant men of the city continued to inspire the support for the Mission on Jefferson Street.[51]

Though the Mission quickly expanded to include additional spheres of ministry beyond Holcombe's preaching, evangelizing and ministering to broken men remained his personal priority. Holcombe's compassion compelled him to provide food and temporary lodging for desperate men who came to his Mission for aid and relief. However, as the profile of the Mission continued to rise, a growing influx of men made it impossible for Holcombe to continue his informal and impromptu acts of charity to all who needed help. Holcombe also worried that undiscerning expressions of charity might encourage a culture of insolence and unwise dependence among the beggars.

Therefore, Holcombe established an additional department of the Mission whereby men might have opportunity to earn their food and lodging in an environment that would expose them to a clear gospel influence. He called this arrangement the "Wayfarer's Rest," and through cooperation with P. Booker Reed, mayor of Louisville 1885 – 1887, and Chief of Police John Henry Whallen, Holcombe was granted the use of a police station building free of rent.[52] A generous gift by J. T. Burghard provided the necessary funding to furnish the building with bunks, a stove, cooking utensils, and bathing facilities.[53] This space provided accommodations for sixty men, assigned to various tasks with an emphasis upon the sawing of kindling wood. Men would labor for an hour to earn either one night's lodging or a meal, while arrangements would be made to sell their wood produce by the superintendent of the Wayfarer's Rest. The income from the wood sales—averaging about ten dollars per day during the winter—funded the salaries of the department's superintendent and book-keeper while daily meals for the working men were donated by the Alexander Hotel Company.[54]

Of this self-supporting ministry, Gross Alexander stated that it became a social model for solving "the vexed question as to the proper treatment of tramps and beggars."[55] Rather than encouraging a culture of dependence or sloth, the Wayfarer's Rest required some participation on the part of the men receiving aid to safeguard against abuses of the system which had plagued some of Holcombe's work in the early years. This approach was especially close to Holcombe's heart, and as Alexander noted: "Mr. Holcombe's experience as a tramp in Colorado leads him to take a brotherly interest in all these unfortunate men."[56]

During these early years of Holcombe's Mission work, he earned the respect of some of the nation's most respected evangelical preachers and evangelists such as Dwight L. Moody and John A. Broadus of The Southern Baptist Theological Seminary, which had relocated its operations to Louisville in 1877. According to the annual catalogs of Southern Seminary, Holcombe enrolled as a student for the 1881 – 1882 academic year, taking classes under Broadus in the New Testament and Homiletics department.[57] He apparently had little time to complete his formal education, however, as he simply attended Broadus' lectures on the same subjects the following year.[58] Holcombe developed a personal kinship with the great Baptist preacher, and Broadus's local support became especially valuable, as Holcombe frequently called upon him to preach to the visitors of the Mission.[59]

Broadus became a mutual friend of both Holcombe and Gross Alexander, which resulted in the Baptist professor contributing a letter of recommendation for Alexander's biography of Holcombe, which saw publication in 1888 by the Press of the *Courier-Journal*.

Broadus spoke approvingly of Holcombe's testimony and evangelistic work, hopeful that the Alexander biography might stir up
Christian compassion in rescue ministry:

> "It is a wonderful story. . . . I think the book will be widely
> read. It will stir Christians to more hopeful efforts to save
> the most wicked. It will encourage many a desperate wan-
> derer to seek the grace of God in the Gospel. Such a book
> makes a real addition to the 'evidences of Christianity.'
> No one can read it without feeling that Christian piety
> is something real and powerful and delightful. Much may
> be learned from Mr. Holcombe's recorded methods and
> discourses, and from the testimonies of his converts, as
> to the best means of carrying on religious work
> of many kinds."[60]

The support of such well-known public figures and preachers
throughout the city and beyond helped grow the reputation of
Holcombe and his Mission. Within less than five years, the Walnut Street Methodist church's Mission had already left a definitive
impression upon the evangelical leaders of Louisville. This rapid
success owed in great part to the remarkable transformative story
of Holcombe himself from one of society's most despicable men
into one of the community's most benevolent visionaries. Since
his conversion, Holcombe had dedicated his life to redeeming
and reforming other wretched men who were in similar straits to
his former life. This same vision attracted the attention of other
men—many with great wealth and influence—from across the
city's evangelical spectrum to see if the Mission might be able to
achieve more ambitious things with a unified evangelical
support structure.

3

THE INCORPORATION OF
THE UNION GOSPEL MISSION

From its humble 1881 beginnings as a church ministry in a vacant store on Jefferson Street, the Mission had been a Methodist endeavor. Since that time, Holcombe and his work increased in reputation across the city. Evangelical churches of diverse denominational persuasions recognized the unique ministry opportunity of the Mission and desired to share in support of the Mission in some official capacity.

EVANGELICAL DIRECTION

On April 11, 1885, the Holcombe Mission took its first decisive step to transform itself into a ministry that would entail a more ambitious identity. In the Y.M.C.A. rooms on Walnut Street, a group of twenty-three Christian men met together for prayer and to outline a plan for incorporating a new incarnation of the Mission. The preface to their official minute book stated the purpose of this conference:

> "The Holcombe Mission which had been founded and conducted since its inception by Fifth and Walnut St. Methodist Episcopal Church South and who had defrayed all expenses &c. incident to maintenance of

Same and who owned the Mission, had been requested to make the scope of the work larger and more general, especially had this been urged upon them by Christian people since the coming among us of the Evangelists Needham, Moody, Whittle, and others whose work like that of Holcombe's had been signally blessed of God. In deference to this wish from the Christian people outside of the Methodist Church this conference had been called. Mr. Jas. G. Carter said that he represented Walnut St. Church and that that church believing that in Unity was strength and that the object sought by them in establishing this Mission viz. the elevating and raising up of those heretofore generally outcasts not only from the church but society, was perhaps better attained by an Union of all Christian denominations that they stood ready providing satisfactory results and arrangements were the outcome of this conference, to turn over the Mission to the Union Gospel Mission which was to include all Evangelical denominations and they henceforth to carry on and control same."[1]

The list of men attending the conference included R. J. Menefee (Chairman), James E. Chilton, James G. Walker, James G. Carter, John A. Carter, T. P. White, Bennett H. Young, James S. Barrett, John G. Barrett, George W. Wicks, J. P. Torbitt, J. W. Akin, Howard W. Hunter, L. Richardson, Frank Miller, J. T. Burghard, A. M. Sea, T. A. Lyon, W. C. Hall, Harry C. Warren, George W. Morris, John L. Wheat, and W. T. Rolph (Secretary).[2] Most of these Christian laymen were also successful businessmen of Louisville; John A. Carter, for instance, was the founder of Carter Dry Goods Co.[3] At the meeting, the men discussed a new constitution for the Holcombe Mission which would accomplish their stated purpose of broadening the Mission's influence towards evangelical churches of a plurality of denominations. They appointed a committee of five—James Barrett, Young, John Carter, Burghard, and Torbitt— to investigate, amend, or revise the proposed constitution and report back to the conference the following week.

One week later, on the evening of April 18, the conference reconvened at the same location to pray and adopt the final draft of the constitution, the text of which is recorded by hand in the official minute book of the Union Gospel Mission.[4]

The constitution stated the objective for the newly named Union Gospel Mission of Louisville was "to do General Gospel City Missionary work to reach the masses, and to provide for the wants of those who need Christian teaching and encouragement." In accordance with its ecumenical management structure, the document stipulated "the management and teaching shall be strictly evangelical and absolutely non-denominational." Its Board of Managers would be self-perpetuating and "composed of one lay-member from each Evangelical Congregation now existing or hereafter established in the City." This Board of Managers would annually designate seven of its members—but no two of the same denomination—to serve on an executive committee that would exercise general control and oversight of the Mission's departments. Each April, the Board must also select members to serve on sub-committees and elect persons to fill the offices of President, Vice-President, Treasurer, and Secretary. Any amendments or alterations to the constitution required a two-thirds vote of the Board of Managers, nine of which were required to constitute a quorum.

Following the adoption of the constitution, the meeting turned its attention to the appointment of its board of managers, which according to their constitution would include one lay-member from each of the city's "evangelical congregations." The Union Gospel Mission's minute book lists sixty recognized congregations entailing Baptist, Christian, Episcopal, Evangelical, Reformed, Methodist, Presbyterian, and Lutheran persuasions. The next week, at an April 25 meeting, the newly elected board members met together for official organization of the Union Gospel Mission. The work of the original committee had concluded with the acceptance of a constitution and election of a managing board. This meeting saw the formal surrendering of the work to the charge of the new board.

On a May 2, 1885 meeting of the Union Gospel Mission's Board of Managers, it elected the first officers: Jonathan A. Carter (a member of the Walnut Street Methodist church) as president, R. J. Menefee (Presbyterian) as vice-president, W. P. Clancy (Baptist) as treasurer, and W. T. Rolph (Methodist) as secretary.[5] Clancy declined his election, and a June 20 meeting of the Board of Managers named P. H. Tapp to hold the office. Rolph served a pivotal role as secretary in the Mission's early days; it was his responsibility to write to all churches to request a lay-member to fill vacancies on the board and to notify all appointed members.[6] Carter, as the newly elected president, then called the board to order after a brief recess so that it could elect an Executive Committee of seven men from across the denominational spectrum; the committee elected J. P. Torbitt (of Walnut Street Christian Church) as its permanent chairman.[7]

At a meeting of the executive committee on May 29, members were elected for fulfillment of the other committees outlined by the UGM constitution. Torbitt, who was already chairman of the executive committee, also became the chair of the Finance Committee's original nine members.[8] L. Richardson chaired the Committee on Location, J. T. Burghard chaired the Committee on Devotion, Harvey T. Irwin chaired the Sunday

School Committee, and P. Meguiar chaired the Industrial School Committee.

In June, the *Courier-Journal* published a notice of the newly constituted Union Gospel Mission after an interview with Carter, who spoke highly of Holcombe's previous years of labor with the Mission under the fold of the Walnut Street Methodist Church:

> "With a desire to assist and convert these dissipated and unfortunate people, who were and are living without God and without hope, Holcombe was put in charge. He has done the work well. He has shown untiring zeal and great efficiency. Through this simple Gospel mission, many souls have been saved, drunkards and gamblers rescued, and homes of misery made happy and prosperous."[9]

Carter explained that the change in management in no way indicated a desire to change the nature of the Mission's general work, but rather to increase its pool of resources to further the work:

> "The Fifth and Walnut Methodist church . . . organized this Holcombe Mission and our church, but principally a few members, have, with the assistance of a few small contributors outside, carried on the work ever since. . . . The change was made because many of the brethren of other denominations desired to join the work, and it is now so organized that all Christian people, in fact all who believe in moral and religious influences, can feel an interest and joint ownership. Then again, under joint management and support, the work can be broadened, a larger field can be opened up, and more good can be done for a distressed class who have a claim upon the Christian community."[10]

Carter also cited the Louisville revivals conducted by prominent evangelists like Dwight L. Moody as a pivotal impetus in bringing the former Holcombe Mission into esteem among the city's evangelical pastors and churches. He estimated that an annual budget of at least $4,000 would be required to sustain the newly constituted Mission, and he encouraged subscriptions towards that end.[11] He invited all interested to persons to see the work firsthand:

> "Now, if you want to witness strange and interesting sights—hear wonderful testimony as to the power of God unto salvation, and see what Brother Holcombe and the Union Gospel Mission are doing—go to the room, south side of Jefferson, between Fourth and Fifth, and take your friends. Then urge all to work for it and give toward its support. Many have gone there doubting the methods adopted, but always leave firm friends. You will have a like experience."[12]

NEW PURPOSE FOR OLD STONES

With growing ambition for the Mission's work to represent the interests of all Louisville's evangelical bodies, a new location became necessary for the advancement of the work. The repurposed gambler's room at 436 Jefferson Street would be inadequate to the grand design which Christian visionaries had for its role in the city. At a January 21, 1886 meeting of the executive committee, a discussion focused upon the propriety of purchasing a lot and mansion located on 128 Jefferson Street, between Brook Street and First Street.[13]

The property under consideration had previously belonged to Benjamin Smith, an affluent Mississippi-Louisiana planter who used the property as a summer home for hosting lively parties for Southern belles and beaux. According to Maude Abner's historical overview of the mansion, the physical structure was likely constructed sometime in the late 1830s by architect John Gwathney.[14] The mansion, described as "massive," consisted of twenty-three rooms and was brick from the basement to the attic, complimented by a "handsome, oval, spiral stairway, the massive hardwood doors, the fine hardware, and the big rooms."[15]

Holcombe played a key role in negotiating the opportunity for purchase. When he became aware that the Smith property was for sale, he immediately recognized the mansion would be suitable for the work of the Mission's various departments. Procuring the keys to inspect the premises, he walked the halls of the spacious stone structure in solitude, pausing in each of its twenty-three rooms to pray that God would give it into his hands for the Mission work. Despite his great faith in God for provision, Holcombe's hope faced an obstacle in the form of a German singing society that was already engaged in negotiations to purchase the building, and it also had greater financial resources available than did the Union Gospel Mission. Holcombe remained undeterred and met with the society's leader to inform him of his ambitions for the former Smith mansion. The response of the society's leader, as recounted by Gross Alexander, is a remarkable testament to how highly regarded was Holcombe's reputation in Louisville, even among those who did not identify as Christians: "Mr. Holcombe, though I am not a Christian and do not believe in Christianity, I do believe in the work you are doing. I will not be in the way of your getting that building." The German singing society withdrew its bid and the directors of the Holcombe Mission were granted a window of opportunity to purchase the property at a price of $12,500.[16]

Though Holcombe had secured a window of opportunity for the Union Gospel Mission to secure the property for a reasonable cost, the Mission needed to act expediently in order to seize the deal. At the January 26 meeting of the executive committee, discussion continued regarding the Smith property, and a consensus emerged that the property would be suitable for the purposes of the Union Gospel Mission. Attention turned to the financial expediency of securing funds for purchasing the property, and motion carried that a sub-committee should be appointed to consider the means of raising the money and the securing of subscriptions from the public.[17]

Within a week, secretary Rolph prepared a circular letter on behalf of the committee by which to announce to the citizens of Louisville that the Mission needed generous donations in order to purchase a suitable permanent home for its work:

> "The Board of Managers, through this committee, now announce to the citizens of Louisville that they have an opportunity of getting just such a place as is in every way suited for the work. They are given the opportunity, for a brief time, to buy at a low price the property known as the Smith property . . . and we now appeal to every person in Louisville to show appreciation of the Mission and its object by raising the sum of twelve thousand dollars, with which amount the purchase can be consummated. . . . the cause a noble one, the time short to take this admirable advantage . . . Will you sustain it? Your answer must be prompt."[18]

On February 3, Holcombe wrote to his friend S. P. Dalton—a convert made through the Mission now living in Cleveland, Ohio—to inform him of the progress in possessing the Smith mansion:

> "Our mission is being abundantly blessed of God, although meeting, from time to time, with those drawbacks which remind us of our dependence and the need of constant prayer. We are having good meetings and conversions are

numerous, and, as a rule of such a character as to make us believe they are genuine and permanent. As I write, our friends are canvassing the city for the collection of means to purchase the old Smith mansion on Jefferson street, for our use, and believing all our work to be of God I have no doubt that it will be ours within a week. Then shall we do a great work for Louisville and for souls. Our sewing school and our Sunday-school, having outgrown our present quarters, will be greatly enlarged and every department of our work also."[19]

As Holcombe indicated in his letter to Dalton, city-wide canvassing became the primary means of raising funds for the Mission's property fund. The Union Gospel Mission's committee meeting on February 5 carried a motion to delegate representatives to canvass various divisions of the city on behalf of raising funds for the Mission.[20] Meanwhile, the Mission had enough funds to move forward within their window of opportunity to possess the property. At the next week's meeting on February 11, it authorized Carter, Torbitt, and Burghard to purchase the Smith property on behalf of the Union Gospel Mission. Furthermore, the committee authorized the same men to prepare articles of incorporation to present to the state legislature.[21]

The city-wide canvassing for subscriptions continued; by March 11, $4,500 had been raised for the Mission. The executive committee appointed a committee to identify persons of means and charitable reputations who might be called upon to contribute generously to the Mission.[22] The Mission also sought to recruit the services of revivalist Sam Jones, who considered Holcombe a dear friend after first meeting him in 1882, to help promote the cause of the Union Gospel Mission by granting the board's members places on his platforms. Jones was unavailable throughout most of

1886, but he later agreed to preach in April 1887 at Holcombe's request.[23]

Jones also wrote Holcombe a word of encouragement regarding the Mission's efforts to secure a suitable permanent home in a March 16 letter:

> "Dear Brother Holcombe: Yours of March 10th received. I thought you were wise enough to know, when you wanted to plant yourself in permanent quarters, that the devil would do his best to prevent it. The devil don't like you anyway; but keep your equilibrium—God is with you; and He is more than all that can be against you."[24]

INCORPORATION OF THE UNION GOSPEL MISSION

On April 1, the Union Gospel Mission became incorporated by enactment of the General Assembly of the Commonwealth of Kentucky. Of special note in the UGM's official charter, is the statement that its purposes of existence necessarily included the preaching of the Christian religion, the Sabbath Schools, and the continuance of religious services and ministries focused especially on the behalf of Louisville residents who were unlikely to frequent the religious services or ministries of the previously established Christian churches and organizations.[25] The charter also affirmed the nondenominational evangelical nature of its Board of Directors, as well as its non-profit status and tax-exempt property.

The full text of the charter is read as follows:

> Be it enacted by the General Assembly of the Commonwealth of Kentucky:

> Section 1. That J. P. Torbitt, John A. Carter, L. Richardson, J. T. Burghard, R. J. Menefee, Arthur Peter, John T.

Moore, John Finzer, J. K. Goodloe, Presley Meguiar, Clinton McClarty, W. T. Rolph, H. V. Loving and their successors in office shall be, and they are hereby constituted a body politic and corporate, to have perpetual succession and to be known by the name and style of "The Union Gospel Mission of Louisville, Kentucky," and by that name shall be competent to contract and be contracted with, to sue and be sued in all courts and places, and in all matters whatever, as natural persons; with full power to acquire by gift, devise, or purchase or otherwise, hold possess, use and occupy, and the same to, sell convey, and dispose of, by exchange or otherwise, all such real estate, goods, effects and chattels as shall be necessary or convenient for the transaction of business and purposes contemplated by said corporation, which business and purposes are, to present and have preached the Christian religion, establish Sabbath Schools and prosecute religious services and efforts in behalf of the residents of the city of Louisville and State of Kentucky, and especially in behalf of those wicked and abandoned men, women and children who do not and will not frequent the ordinary houses of worship, and the ordinary religious services and Christian instruction offered in the now established Churches, Sabbath Schools and Missions, and said corporation may have and use a Common Seal and change, alter and renew the same at pleasure; and may ordain and put into execution all such by-laws, rules and regulations for the conduct and management of the same, as may be deemed convenient or necessary to the welfare and success of the business and purposes thereof. The property of said corporation, whilst used for the purposes of conducting its said business and purposes, shall be exempt from all taxes, whether State, County or Municipal.

Section 2. Said corporation shall be under the control of the members of the various evangelical denominations of Christians in Louisville, Kentucky, and the first Board of Directors thereof shall consist of the corporators before mentioned to serve until their successors shall be elected and enter upon their duties.

Section 3. The number of directors, time of elections thereof, by whom, and for what time elected, shall be determined by the by-laws of the Corporation to be adopted after the organization under the Charter, and said Corporation may change its by-laws as may therein be provided.

Section 4. There shall be no capital stock of said Corporation. The terms and duration of membership in said Corporation shall be fixed by the by-laws and the filling of all vacancies in the Board of Directors shall also be provided for by the by-laws, and such by-laws may extend to all matters concerning the welfare, management and conduct of said Corporation, as provided in the first section of this Charter, which are not inconsistent therewith; or with the Constitution and laws of this State and of the United States.

Section 5. All property and all money derived from memberships in said Corporation, or by gift or devise, shall be devoted exclusively to promoting the business and purposes and to the success thereof.

Section 6. This act shall take effect and be in force from its passage.[26]

The Smith property became legally deeded to the Mission on April 9, 1886. On April 15, the Union Gospel Mission established its official by-laws, outlining the titles and duties of its officers. The board authorized Vice-President Menefee to examine the property and have it insured in any way he deemed necessary.[27] Holcombe, who a few months earlier had walked and prayed in each of the mansion's twenty-three rooms, now experienced the joy of hope rewarded. He repurposed the building to suit the needs of the Mission's departments. He fitted the rooms of the lower level for the various departments and his office, the parlors he converted into a single large room capable of seating over two-hundred people, and the seven rooms of the second floor became the lodging quarters for Holcombe's family.[28]

Holcombe wrote to Dalton to inform him that the Mission had purchased its new home and had plans to open services there around May:

> "Our work is moving like a thing of life. It was never so prosperous before.... Sister Clark [superintendent of the Industrial School] is in her glory. She is one of the grandest Christian women I have ever seen. Nearly all the converts are doing well."[29]

The Mission's Board of Directors met April 27 to crystallize the terms of serving on said board, as well as the position of pastor-in-charge and the standing committees.[30] The directors nominated and affirmed Holcombe as the pastor-in-charge for the year to "control the preaching and other religious labors of the institution ... subject to the supervision and direction of the Executive Committee."[31] Elections to one-year terms of service on the board of directors were scheduled annually on the first Tuesday of April.[32] The terms of service required that at least one board member be named whose church membership belonged to a congregation of the recognized evangelical denominations of Louisville: Presbyterian Church North, Presbyterian Church South, Baptist, Lutheran, the Christian Church, Methodist Church South, Methodist Church North, Episcopal, and Cumberland Presbyterian Church. The board's responsibility would be to ensure representation of all the city's evangelical denominations in the Mission's standing committees and their respective chairmen. Memberships on each of the standing committees—as well as the pastorate position—were one-year terms of service to be filled at the discretion of the Board of Directors at its annual meeting on the first Tuesday in April.

The memberships of the standing committees were generally reduced from the original 1885 constitution. The Mission's Executive Committee now consisted of three members—Torbitt, Menefee, and Peter—rather than nine, selected from the Board of Directors, with no two being from the same denomination, to exercise the full authority of the board over all the Union Gospel Mission's departments, with the board president being an ex-officio member.[33] The Finance Committee reduced from nine to five members, with three constituting a quorum. The Committee on Devotion reduced from five to three with a quorum of two. Having secured the Smith property as the Mission's permanent location, the House and Grounds Committee superseded the functions of the former committee on location and rooms.[34]

By May 20, the Mission had raised between $7,000 and $8,000 for the building fund through their canvassing efforts, although they continued to publicize their needs for more subscriptions to pay off the remainder of their property debt.[35] The Mission fixed Holcombe's salary as superintendent at $1,000 annually.[36] As 1886 drew near its end, the Union Gospel Mission found work copacetic in the new mansion. Holcombe wrote again to his friend Dalton informing him that:

> "Our work is more quiet now. The papers do not notice it so much, but we are doing a good work. It is now more among the unfortunate business men of the city some of whom were fallen very low. Some who have recently been reclaimed are now first-class business men. The old converts are all right and doing well, but they don't stand by me in the work as I wish they would."[37]

For Holcombe, the sense of quietness was soon shattered by a near tragedy. On a Sunday afternoon in January 1887, he encountered an intruder on the mansion's second floor, where his family kept their living quarters. Holcombe questioned the stranger during an increasingly tense exchange, which ended with Holcombe chasing the intruder out of the house. A few hours later, however, the intruder returned to the mansion with two other accomplices, impersonating police officers. As Holcombe questioned the men's credentials, the three men attacked him and broke his leg before fleeing the scene of the crime.[38]

This attack confined Holcombe to bed rest for over a month. During his period of recuperation, an outpouring of support proved the degree of esteem with which the city of Louisville held its famous gambler turned mission worker. Alexander records the great outpouring of support from across the spectrum of social classes:

> "On Monday, the day following his misfortune, Mr. Holcombe's room was nearly all the day long, full of people of every grade from the mayor and the richest and finest

people on Broadway and Fourth avenue, down to the poor drunkard and outcast, who forgot his shabby dress and pressed in among those fine people in order to see 'Brother Holcombe,' and find out how he was. The ministers of the leading churches of every Protestant denomination came with words of sympathy and prayer.... And Mr. Holcombe lay in his bed and wept—not for pain, but for gratitude and humble joy. 'Why,' said he, 'I would be willing to have half a dozen legs broken to know that these people think so much of me and my poor efforts to be useful.' "[39]

In the same month, the Mission's directors established an emergency fund of twenty dollars from which Holcombe would be able to draw from the Treasurer each month. The Mission benefited from the public endorsements of great revivalist preachers like Sam P. Jones and D. L. Moody in raising awareness of its work. The Mission's board encouraged Holcombe—who had a special rapport with both men—to implore the preachers to make local visits and show their solidarity with the ministry.[40] Jones consented to preach April 10 at Macauley's Theatre on the Mission's behalf, which still needed about seven thousand more dollars to pay off the property debt and fund its necessary expenses. A public letter from the directors encouraged all Louisville to turn out for Jones's meeting for the good of the Union Gospel Mission:

"We appeal to Christians and all charitably disposed citizens to give Mr. Jones a liberal response. He comes in the goodness of his heart to preach the Gospel and to ask your help in sustaining an organization whose aim is to lift the fallen, encourage the unfortunate and save those who are without hope. May we not expect all who attend this meeting will come with warm hearts and open hands?" [41]

The Mission's financial resources continued to be tight, even as the city canvassing continued. In September, Mrs. Clark of the kindergarten department successfully petitioned the Board of Directors to start a training school for kindergarten teachers who would be deployed across the city; Clark sought no additional financial aid for the expanded services, asking simply for the board's cooperation and advice.[42] Clark sacrificed personal comforts in order to pay for kindergarten teacher salaries out of her own pocket, and President Carter and his wife opened their own home to board Anna Bryan who would serve as superintendent of the department for some years and train other workers. By November, the department had incorporated itself into the Louisville Free Kindergarten Association.[43]

THE RESIGNATION OF HOLCOMBE

The minutes of the Mission directors' meeting of November 23, 1887 record an incident that may evidence the impetus of a growing rift between Holcombe and the Mission's Board. While in New York, Holcombe incurred an expense of $40 without prior approval from the board. Although the board authorized the treasurer to reimburse Holcombe the expense, it resolved that "hereafter the Board will not assume or pay any such subscription without their express authority in advance."[44] Furthermore, the Mission directors voted to abolish the emergency fund previously established in January which had granted Holcombe the freedom to withdraw a maximum of $20 per month. The board now expressed its belief that said fund "was not a helping but a hindrance to the work," although the minutes explicitly stated that "this repeal is in no sense a reflection upon Bro. Holcombe."[45]

The next recorded meeting of the Mission Board of Directors also resulted in some contentious business. This meeting centered upon the Wayfarer's Rest ministry which had been started by Holcombe and heavily supported by J. T. Burghard in 1885. This ministry received great attention for allowing destitute men an outlet to work for housing and food, and had been self-sustaining through the sale of the men's produce.[46] Holcombe and W. C. Priest, who had served on the Committee of House and Grounds, brought a request to the board regarding the usage of Mission grounds for the Wayfarer's Rest program.[47] The January 25, 1888 minutes record that "a long discussion occurred as to the granting of privilege of part of grounds and some members of committee left ere vote was taken, when it was so taken on question of granting them use of certain portions of yard it resulted in tie vote chairman voting which was excepted to. The matter was then left in status quo for further consideration and meeting adjourned."[48] At the next week's meeting, the fallout over the Wayfarer's Rest continued with the resignation of Burghard from the Board of Directors and as chairman of the Devotional Committee; the board accepted his resignation "with regret."[49]

D. L. Moody preached a revival in Louisville in January and February of 1888, and bestowed his approval upon the work of the Mission with an appeal for the city to support the work:

> "I have got very much interested in a work in your city conducted by a man you call Steve Holcombe. I don't know when I met a man who so struck my heart. I went up and saw his headquarters and how he works. He is doing the noblest work I know of. I want you to help him with money and words of cheer. Remember here in Louisville you make so many drunkards that you must have a place to take care of the wrecks. Steve Holcombe rescues them. Let us help him all we can."[50]

The Union Gospel Mission minutes for February 16 gratefully acknowledged "Mr. Moody's effort and work to raise debt on building."[51]

In April 1888, the annual elections for Mission's directors, officers and committee members took place as stipulated by the charter. Discussion also continued regarding the prudency of Holcombe's emergency fund, with President Carter and Treasurer Tapp granted power to act upon any financial requests, so long as funds paid did not exceed $20 per month.[52] The Union Gospel Mission continued to tread water financially, although necessary maintenance on the property demanded large expenses. In November, the directors extended another circular letter to friends and donors requesting additional emergency contributions for "necessary repairs on the home of the Mission in order to preserve it from decay."[53]

At a July 17 meeting, Holcombe addressed the board regarding the possibility of a Professor Togg of Frankfort, Kentucky to take charge of the music ministry for the Mission's regular services. The Mission board requested Holcombe write Togg to ascertain whether he might be able to receive compensation outside the resources of the Mission. The board initially determined not to entertain any arrangement in which Togg would become a tenant of the Mission house. Immediately, a motion to reconsider the decision was moved and carried, resulting in a loosening of the board's previous absolutist position on Togg's potential tenancy. Another motion carried instructing Holcombe to report back to the board as to names of any other candidates for the teaching of music that would be willing to accept the work.[54] Ultimately, Holcombe and the Mission board settled on pursuing the services of another man and his wife to have charge of the music ministry at a salary of $20 per month.[55]

At the April 2, 1889 meeting of the Board of Directors, it discussed a proposition as to whether the stable of the Mission property might be leased to certain parties. The directors declined the proposition as being foreign to the Mission's charter, and that the reception of rent payment might jeopardize its tax exempt status. The board also elected H. V. Loving to the office of treasurer upon the resignation of Tapp, who had served in that position since 1885.[56] Tapp's retirement resulted in a lengthy letter of appreciation drafted by Rolph for his years of service, but the most significant change to the Union Gospel Mission came later that year.

On August 27, 1889, Holcombe submitted his resignation to the directors of the Union Gospel Mission.[57] The handwritten letter read:

> "I have after long and prayerful consideration of the subject been brought to the conclusion that my work at the Mission is about at an end, and that some other can take it at this point and do more than I can to advance the cause.
>
> I therefore beg leave to offer my resignation to take effect the first of October, the end of the year for which I agreed to work. During the time of my connection with the Mission you have been exceedingly kind to me for all of which I must earnestly thank you, and I pray that you may be guided in the selection of a man to take charge who will have great success in the work. I shall continue to devote myself to Christian work in whatever way Providence may show me but I am satisfied that the time has come for the work of the Mission to be turned over to somebody else.
>
> Whatever I can do to aid in the work without being officially connected with it, I shall be glad to do.
>
> Yours fraternally,
> Steve P. Holcombe"

The Mission's directors received and accepted Holcombe's resignation at its September 20 meeting. With great regret, the board wrote Holcombe a letter of appreciation for all his labors:

"Dear Sir & Brother:
In accepting your voluntary resignation as Pastor of Union Gospel Mission, which you have held since its first start some five years ago, the Directors of same desire to express to you their sincere regrets at such separation, brought about as it is by your own desire entirely and the belief on your part that a still more useful field of labor is before you. That this may be realized for you is our earnest and heartfelt wish and in that case our present great loss will be the Master's and your gain. We are however constrained to say that we have regarded the union of yourself and the Mission as one that only death could have severed. The name of Holcombe Mission and the blessed association connected therewith will be remembered as long as the Mission stands.

We can even now scarcely realize that you who labored 'in Season and out of Season' so faithfully and earnestly in this vineyard of the Lord and have been blessed in seeing the fruits thereof and whose name in connection with this work is known far beyond the bounds of our State, will leave us to enter new fields, but 'He who ruleth all things well' and has had you in his keeping knows best and 'chooses our changes for us' will cause 'all things to work together for good for those who love him.'

In bidding you God-speed in your work accept from us this testimony of our high appreciation of your noble Christian character, your fidelity and zeal to the cause of the Master, and permit us to wish you an abundant success

in every undertaking and health and happiness to yourself
and family. We are in Christian love.
Your Friends and Brethren"[58]

The Mission's Board then turned its attention toward the seemingly impossible task of replacing Holcombe as pastor of the
Mission, which had become practically synonymous with the
famous testimony of the converted gambler. Whatever reasons
might have incited Holcombe's resignation from the Mission,
primary source documents indicate genuine Christian respect and
goodwill that both parties still possessed for one another. Over the
following years, however, the relations between Holcombe and the
Union Gospel Mission directors would not continue to evidence
the same charitable consensus. Without Holcombe's presence, the
Mission would find it increasingly difficult to garner financial
support and maintain its chartered purposes of organization.

4

THE HOLCOMBE LEGACY

Having received Holcombe's resignation letter on September 20, 1889, the Union Gospel Mission's Board of Directors immediately turned its attention to filling the vacated position of pastor. It appointed a committee—consisting of J. P. Torbitt, Arthur Peter, R. J. Menefee, W. T. Rolph, and President John A. Carter—to find a suitable replacement who could also occupy the mansion as a permanent resident.[1] By October, the committee determined that the Mission should pursue Rev. John M. Philips, of Newport, Kentucky, as the candidate to succeed Holcombe. Philips visited Louisville to meet with a portion of the directors and spoke three nights at the Mission. He left a favorable impression upon the directors, who noted him as "certainly an excellent and forcible preacher and has a thorough knowledge of the Scriptures."[2]

After three days of preaching and meeting, Philips remained uncertain about accepting the position, expressing his desire to the committee that "he would wait upon the Lord's guidance."[3] The pastoral search committee believed him to be their man, and they recommended his name as the preferred choice to the Mission's Board of Directors. At a specially called meeting of the directors on December 5, the board accepted the unanimous recommendation of the committee and authorized Rolph to write Philips offering him the position of Mission superintendent at an annual salary of $1,000 in addition to compensation for necessary living expenses.[4] Philips accepted and relocated to Louisville to oversee the Mission's preaching responsibilities and other ministry departments.

WEIGHTY MANTLE

Fundraising for the Mission's expenses continued to be a great challenge, and now it faced an even more uncertain future seeking financial support without the asset of Holcombe's immediate presence and widespread popularity. The directors deemed a wise course of action toward this means to target fifty individuals who were not already regular subscribers to the Mission to contribute $25 each to the Union Gospel Mission.[5] The letters were mailed out in March, 1890, both informing the people that Philips now occupied the former seat of Holcombe and of the uniqueness of the Mission's work as being "of a nature entirely outside what the Church is doing," and as such "should receive the hearty support of all who are in a position to aid Christian and philanthropic effort."[6] The distributed letter made clear that the Mission had urgent need for money, and that fifty gifts of $25 in combination with the regular subscriptions should be sufficient to fund the annual expenses and make necessary repairs on the property.

In September of 1890, W. T. Burghard—who had previously resigned two years earlier—briefly rejoined the Mission's Board of Directors. After this election, Burghard almost immediately accepted a position in New York to direct mission work. Burghard's service and financial generosity had been a great asset to both Holcombe and the Union Gospel Mission, and now the Mission had to proceed without his presence and support.[7] The Mission continued to petition their subscribers and the public for funding, pointing attention to its history of success in influencing outcasts of society to become respected men of the community and dedicated heads of families. It praised its Kindergarten Association which "morally and intellectually elevated" the city's lowest classes of children beyond the advantages of their home life.[8] However, generosity no longer followed as liberally as it did under Holcombe's administration.

As a consequence of dwindling public support for the Mission, the directors decided on February 27, 1891 to suspend active work of the Union Gospel Mission effective April 1 of that year, as there was no longer available funding to pay the salary of Philips. R. J. Menfee and John T. Moore resigned from the Board of Directors. The meeting's minutes noted the suspension came about "in view of the want of interest existing in this community to the work of the Union Gospel Mission and our consequent inability to secure the funds necessary to its adequate support."[9] The directors, in dismissing the services of Philips as pastor and superintendent, communicated to him "the high esteem of the Board for his work and our confidence in his earnest Christian character and zeal in the cause of the Master."[10]

The directors agreed that the active work of the Mission could not resume until it could be done with financial sustainability, therefore they sought no replacement superintendent or pastor-in-charge to succeed Philips. By May 12, the Mission only had $64.30 in its treasury. Other ministers in the city desired to make use of the empty rooms of the Mission's mansion. The board minutes for the May 12 meeting record a discussion about the expediency of an application by a Rev. Bristol to occupy some of the rooms.[11] In October, T. T. Eaton—influential pastor of Louisville's Walnut Street Baptist Church and editor of the *Western Recorder*—applied to make use of the Mission's facilities for about eight months, but the directors declined his request as being contrary to the chartered purpose of the Union Gospel Mission.[12]

The kindergarten ministry remained the silver lining in the cloud hanging over the Union Gospel Mission in 1891, as it continued to meet in the mansion and spawned many similar schools. By this time, the Kindergarten Association was rapidly maturing into its own institution and continued to make use of the UGM facilities as a convenience. The Board of Directors' September minutes noted the Louisville Free Kindergarten would be required to pay for half of the Mission's coal bill.[13]

At the directors' March 18, 1892 meeting, the minutes record that President Carter presented a November 17, 1891 letter from Holcombe which was read before the attendees. The directors ordered a "reply sent in the appropriate way" to Holcombe courtesy of Secretary Rolfe. The minutes do not include a copy of the text of Holcombe's letter, but a discussion followed regarding the current state of the Mission in preparation for its 1892 annual meeting to be held the following month.[14] Little business occurred at the annual directors' meeting on April 5, as the Mission had less than five dollars in its treasury.[15]

THE RETURN OF HOLCOMBE

By May of 1893, Holcombe desired to return to the Union Gospel Mission to oversee the preaching ministry. His daughter Mayme Holcombe wrote a formal request on his behalf to President Carter that Steve Holcombe be permitted to return to his former post and for the Holcombe family to receive lodging at the Mission's property. A specially called meeting of the directors was held on May 12 to consider the request, but the directors ultimately denied it due to lack of confidence in the public interest to support the financial demands of a superintendent's salary. The directors authorized Secretary Rolph to return correspondence explaining the directors' position. Rolph's response letter to Miss Holcombe stated:

> "The Board, after due consideration of the matter, finds itself in a position to be unable at this time to offer any encouragement with the view of opening the Mission, for the reason that the general public have not assisted them in this particular. Hence, it had to cease, and will have to remain so until the Public feel warranted in sustaining and supporting the Mission in a way that they do not now seem to care to. The Directors had put up their money to support it until they tired of it."[16]

Rolph's letter proceeded to state that "The Mission house is occupied at the present time and work is going on in all branches except in so far as mission and preaching services for men."[17] From Steve Holcombe's perspective, this arrangement was unsatisfactory and a violation of the chartered purpose of the Union Gospel Mission. He proceeded to sue the Mission's directors to reinstate the preaching services in accordance with its chartered purpose. Section 1 of the charter stated clearly that the Mission "shall be competent to contract and be contracted with, to sue and be sued in all courts and places, and in all matters whatever, as natural persons . . . which business and purposes are, to present and have preached the Christian religion, establish Sabbath Schools and prosecute religious services and efforts in behalf of the residents of the city of Louisville and State of Kentucky, and especially in behalf of those wicked and abandoned men."[18]

The legal effects of Holcombe's challenge culminated in February 1894, when the directors surrendered their interest in the Union Gospel Mission to their legal successors.[19] Sometime after his 1889 resignation from the Union Gospel Mission, Holcombe had started his own ministry under the name of "The Holcombe Mission," which had its own board of directors. The directors of the Union Gospel Mission met with George H. Simmons, W. M. Danner and George P. Kendrick—the president, secretary and treasurer of the Holcombe Mission's board respectively—to discuss the situation. The three officers of the Holcombe Mission claimed they had no involvement in the party pursuing the lawsuit and, furthermore, were not even aware of its existence until being informed second-hand by one of their fellow directors, S. P. Walker, who was also a lead plaintiff pressing the matter before the Jefferson Circuit Court. The UGM directors hoped to make peace out of court and convince Holcombe's party to withdraw the suit. To that end, they arranged to meet with the plaintiffs of the Holcombe Mission and their attorney to discuss an alternative arrangement; if the Holcombe party would dismiss their suit, then the directors would consequently surrender their trust in the Union Gospel Mission and arrange a transfer of management to their successors.[20]

Holcombe's party and their attorney agreed to such an arrangement; their attorney Elijah S. Watts agreed to dismiss the lawsuit on account of the fact that the purpose of the suit was "to have the Mission run as originally designed."[21] Subsequently, the Union Gospel Mission directors made arrangements to transfer the managerial duties. By request of the board, the official minute book of February 23 noted the directors left the Mission and its property free of all debt and again stated the reasoning for ceasing the regular preaching ministry on account of a lack of funding, while the other departments of Kindergarten, Industrial School, and Sunday School had continued in health.[22] Later that afternoon, six directors formally resigned and appointed the directors of the Holcombe Mission as their rightful successors.[23] The officers—Torbitt, Rolph, and Carter—resigned their posts at the following meeting.[24] Carter, who along with his brother James, had taken the most proactive role in behalf of the Mission since its 1881 inception than anyone else besides Holcombe, having been members of the Walnut Street Methodist Church which had formerly been the sole supports of the work.[25] Upon his resignation, the record book states that he expressed his abiding interest in the Mission "and wished the new Board abundant success and prosperity."[26]

The Mission's new Board of Directors immediately held its first meeting to elect new officers; S. P. Walker became the new president of the board and Holcombe officially resumed his duties as super-intendent of the Union Gospel Mission.[27] The new regime now had to concern itself with fundraising in order to avoid the dire financial state which had besieged the previous administration; they resumed the old tradition of canvassing the city for donations, with hope that the personal presence of Holcombe would instill confidence in donations to the work.[28] The impetus fell upon the directors themselves to raise the money, although the funds remained tight and administrative leadership lacked stability; some of the directors who had carried over from Holcombe's previous mission ministry—George Simmons among them—resigned within about a year of taking over the Union Gospel Mission's affairs; however, Holcombe's old friend J. T. Burghard, who had served for years in the prior administration, did return to the Board of Directors in March of 1895.[29]

In order to build stronger ties with its contributors, the Mission published a sixteen-page annual report in early 1895, illustrating the means and results of its work from the last six months of 1894. The pamphlet reaffirmed the Mission's commitments to its evan-gelical, non-denominational identity and its essential ministries of nightly gospel preaching, the afternoon Sunday School, and the Industrial School for poor children, as well as additional meetings for mothers, converts, and prayer meetings. The report claimed a total attendance of 14,328 at its nightly evangelistic meetings, thirty-six persons sheltered in the Mission's facilities, over 6,000 meals served to guests, and average attendances in excess of ninety persons for both the Sunday School and the Industrial School.[30] The report also appealed for donations, noting that the previous year's work had been accomplished on only $1,800 with Holcombe compensated at half his regular monthly salary, while a full year's worth of work would require raising at least $3,000.[31] The pamphlet also made a plea for additional funds that could be utilized for cast-off clothing, bedding, shoes, food, coal, and vital upgrades to the physical facility, such as removing an interior wall to enlarge the chapel and accommodate growth.[32] Beyond the simple statistics, the pamphlet claimed that:

> "The results of these labors can better be seen than told. It is impossible to give any adequate or accurate idea of the work accomplished or the results attending to our efforts to clothe the naked, feed the hungry, shelter the homeless, and above all else implant in each heart a love of God and a sincere desire to turn away from those things which had brought them to the low estate in which we found them, and point them to Christ, who alone, in spite of all philanthropy, all philosophy, and all else, can reach the sinner and give to him that peace and content which 'passes understanding.' "[33]

Furthermore, the Mission pointed to the fact that they not only worked to redeem people from sin but to also help them onto the path of life reform:

> "Men with God-given gifts, fitted by nature and attainments to be useful members of society, but who, through the bondage of sin, have been brought to the very gutters,

have by the grace of God been reclaimed and restored to friends and to society. Some of these men are to-day occupying positions of trust and profit. Women, unfortunate and sinning, have had peace spoken to their souls, and are now living Christian lives. Youths who had not yet tasted the bitter fruit of sin and young girls with their lives yet unfolded have sought Christ and taken Him as their guide and protector; men and women of all ages and all conditions have acknowledged Him 'Lord of All.' Most of our converts have proved faithful, though among the wheat has been found some chaff."[34]

DIMINISHING RETURNS

During the years of 1895-1896, Holcombe labored as superintendent of the Mission and continued to try and raise funds, sometimes working on the promise of back salary to be paid at a later time. By June of 1896, Holcombe's back pay for services rendered amounted to $1,844.15 when the directors finally reimbursed him; Holcombe voluntarily donated 244.15 of that total back to the Mission.[35] Early in the month, Holcombe wrote to Thomas D. Osborne—a member of Broadway Baptist Church who had succeeded S. P. Walker as president of the Board of Directors in 1896—stating that he had "thought much about how much it would take to live respectfully and kept out of debt" and consequently required at least $75 a month in salary to cover his personal expenses; the Mission honored his request and fixed his salary at that amount on June 26.[36]

In the spring of 1896, Osborne led the Mission's directors to consider the possibility of cooperating in social settlement work with the Louisville High School Alumnae at the Union Gospel Mission. The Social Settlement movement had gained momentum in the late 1880s as an alternative to traditional notions about

charitable services. Rather than simply give temporary aid to society's destitute—which, more often than not, appeased the
philanthropic conscience more than actually bettering the social
condition—social settlements of that era aspired to promote a
social mingling of classes for the purpose of promoting a culture
of mutual respect and cooperation.[37]

Osborne gauged the interest of the Louisville High School
Alumnae regarding possible cooperation in hopes of advancing its
education and evangelistic work while also ensuring additional
funding to keep the building operational. Under the agreement,
the Mission's rooms would have hosted social settlement workers,
while the High School Alumnae would pay the Mission at least
one thousand dollars for maintenance and amenities such as heat
and water. On March 23, Osborne drafted his proposal for a cooperative agreement and submitted it to Sarah Webb Maury, chairman
of the High School Alumnae's Philanthropy Committee, but Maury
declined his proposition.[38] The Alumnae's terms of a proposed
social settlement would have required their organization taking
complete control of the building's facilities rather than reporting
to the accountability of the Mission's directors. A union would
have also required Holcombe to resign as superintendent in favor
of Archibald A. Hill assuming authority to develop the settlement
according to his needs.[39]

The end of the 1896 financial year ultimately resulted in a net
profitability of about $200 for the Mission after expenses, which
was applied to the superintendent salary. Holcombe's work for
the year included organizing a Gospel Meeting every night with
a total attendance of 17,226, nine professed conversions, almost
600 prayer requests, and over 1,000 men received temporary aid
while looking for employment. The combined attendance of the
Sunday School, Industrial School, and other ministries
exceeded 7,000.[40]

Holcombe continued as Mission superintendent for the next ten years, with Osborne continuing as president of the director board. Sadly, official records of the director meetings from this period appear to have been lost to history. One reason for this may have owed to the fact that the directors were not able meet regularly on account of lacking a sufficient quorum due to sickness, death, and removals among the directors.[41] Holcombe worked tirelessly to not only attend to the Mission's preaching ministry, but also to solicit subscriptions and donations on behalf of the institution.[42] Though financial resources remained tight, the Mission persevered and its income managed to exceed its expenses. By 1902, Holcombe's monthly salary had increased to $100, and his yearly financial report to Osborne expressed his gratitude in a financial surplus with optimism that future years would continue to see increased profitability and activity in the Mission's work.[43] Superintendent reports for August through November of that year evidence that Holcombe continued to conduct the gospel services nightly at the Mission, with an average attendance of around twenty persons per meeting, with dozens of persons requesting prayer and professing conversion each month. Other ministries, such as the Sunday School, struggled due to the lack of a permanent superintendent.[44]

In 1903, Holcombe took on an assistant at the Union Gospel Mission, Mrs. Elizabeth M. Cardwell. Cardwell was a widow, whose bereavement over the loss of her husband ultimately drew her to saving faith in Christ, even though she had been an unconverted church member and Sunday School teacher. Cardwell learned about Holcombe's Mission while visiting Louisville, and was so drawn to the ministry that she applied for work immediately. The Mission's physical condition at this point was not an inviting place, as Cardwell described it as "a miserable dark place," although she sensed the Lord leading her to do work providentially prepared. Cardwell met Holcombe in the hallway and expressed her desire "to be of service and a blessing to others, and a willingness to prove it."[45]

Cardwell recounted Holcombe's response from memory to be "Mrs. Cardwell, I had said I would never have another woman assist me. They have all proven to be cranks, but you impress me as being different. I would like to employ you but I haven't the money. How much would you be willing to work for?" Cardwell offered her services in return for only five dollars a month, as she had little desire for any material possessions other than those she already carried on her person. Holcombe, taken aback by her simple request, agreed to employ her at a compensation of three times as much.[46]

Holcombe's alleged comment as to all previous women assistants beings "cranks" gives the appearance of an uncharitable estimation of previous female workers at the Mission. It is curious as to how much he could have meant such an estimation considering such high regard for women like Mrs. J. R. Clark whose services in the early years of the kindergarten department proved invaluable.[47] Whatever the meaning of his remark, Holcombe correctly estimated Cardwell's devotion to the work, as she would remain at the Mission for nearly thirty years.

Cardwell's memories provide a far more vivid picture of Holcombe's work and preaching at the Mission in 1903 than the statistical details preserved in the directors' records:

> "Mr. Holcombe was conducting services every night, which were attended almost exclusively by men. As he faced these cold, hungry men of the street—desperate men—he would bluntly say, 'Suppose these walls would cave in. Where would you be? Where would your soul go?' These curt remarks would often drive their lost condition home to these men. While he talked to them the aroma of good coffee was wafted from the kitchen. The coffee was pre-

pared by putting it into clean, white sacks and dropping them into a large wash boiler of boiling water. The meat and bread sandwiches were served from the boiler top. Trays were soon substituted. The coffee was served in pint tin cups. As I looked out upon the sea of upturned faces, from my seat on the platform and almost hidden by the large organ, I thought I had never seen a more pitiful sight. Escaped convicts, drunkards, highway robbers, drug addicts—all of them badly in need of a friend."[48]

HOLCOMBE'S GREATEST INVESTMENT YIELDS INTEREST

In November 1905, Steve and Mary Holcombe celebrated their fiftieth wedding anniversary with an all-day reception at the Mission.[49] Considering the rocky circumstances into which both partners entered into the marital union in 1855, the endurance of their union for a half-century must be considered a small miracle in itself. Neither one of them were converted Christians at that time, and neither partner's parents approved of the marriage. Furthermore, Steve's love for intoxicating drink and gambling made him prone to wander far away from home; during those precious few times when he did reside at home, he was often unpleasant company for Mary and their children

Since Steve's conversion in late 1877, the entire Holcombe family experienced remarkable transformation. Their son William, who had played an important role in convincing his father to abandon alcoholic beverages and reintroduce him to church ministry, had married in addition to becoming a hard-working employee and churchman who now lived in Indiana. Of their three living daughters, Pearl and Irene had married while Mayme lived in Elizabethtown and had labored with her father in various ways with the Union Gospel Mission.[50] Thomas Osborne arranged the twelve-hour program to honor the Holcombe marriage on November 7, inviting over one hundred friends representing some of Louisville's most prominent family names.[51] This anniversary was yet another opportunity for the friends and admirers of Holcombe and his work to express their gratitude for his legacy of work on behalf of the Mission and his decades of fidelity to the bride who became his long-suffering wife.

The same month, the Union Gospel Mission made plans to change its name to "The Holcombe Mission," to honor its longtime superintendent and, perhaps, with hopes of making the Mission's ties to its famous founder more public in the interest of fundraising. Osborne mailed various notices toward said purpose to Louisville's evangelical churches for approval, and the surviving returned notices suggest most of the churches approved the strategy.[52] The Mission's official letterheads from November, 1905 reflected the change, although the name did not stick for long before reverting back to Union Gospel Mission, for reasons unclear.[53]

The following summer, Holcombe—fast approaching the age of seventy-one—resigned his position of superintendent of the Union Gospel Mission for the second and final time. After twenty-five years of involvement of gospel mission work in Louisville, he sensed the time had come to pass the mantle onto younger workers. Holcombe cited both his advanced age and the diminishing effectiveness of the Mission under his tenure as reasons for the decision:

> "For the last few years, I saw that the mission was not working out as well as it had done formerly. When we started, we were the first in the South and there were only two or three others in the country. Many tramps came here, and were fed and sent on their way with an idea of religion, a new suit of clothes, a full stomach, and a rejuvenated feeling of hopefulness. Soon other missions began

to spring up, and the spirit of competition began to arise. Each one offered the knights of the road more tempting conditions than the others, and soon the men became mere beggars, relying on the missions along their line of march to feed and clothe them. I saw that we were ruining them and the spirit of our undertaking, and I stopped giving them anything but one meal perhaps, and some spiritual advice."[54]

The Union Gospel Mission directors promoted Elizabeth Cardwell, after three years of assisting Holcombe, as the new superintendent, with Holcombe's glowing endorsement, proclaiming her "the most capable person for the task before her that I know of."[55] The transition became official on July 1, 1906.[56] Holcombe retired to his farm in Elizabethtown, Kentucky, although he publically expressed his interest in keeping in contact with Cardwell and maintaining a watchful eye over the work, noting that "The Mission is my child. . . . and I will always watch over it like a fond father."[57] As Holcombe prepared to retire to his farm with Mary, the Union Gospel Mission prepared for harvesting new mission fields under the stewardship of Cardwell.

5

NEW FIELDS
FOR THE HARVEST

Upon his retirement in 1906, Holcombe cast his vision for a new age of ministry for the Union Gospel Mission in a June 24 interview with Louisville's leading newspaper, the *Courier-Journal*:

> "The Steve Holcombe Mission is now a thing of the past, and in its place will arise one of the greatest institutions south of the Ohio River, and one whose need Louisville has felt for many years. Mrs. Elizabeth M. Cardwell, of Lebanon, Ky., will arrive Tuesday to take charge of the old building at First and Jefferson streets, where so many wanderers have found shelter, and will immediately begin preparations to start the new mission working. We are in the center of a large foreign population, especially Italian, and the children are running through the streets without any restraint whatever. Their condition is shocking to the last degree, and they are ill-fed, ill-clothed and untrained. They grow up to be drags on the community instead of able-bodied and helpful citizens."[1]

In 1912, Thomas D. Osborne reflected back upon his first ten years of involvement with the Mission—essentially the time between Holcombe's return and his second retirement—as a time of great struggle. The Board of Directors held very few meetings, and although Holcombe continued to preach and minister, other ministry departments suffered neglect due to tightness of funds. Osborne remarked:

> "When Mr. Holcombe retired and Mrs. Cardwell succeeded it was necessary to revive the Gospel services, the Prayer services also the Industrial School and Sunday School and as the occasion demanded and the opportunity presented itself and funds were available additional services were added."[2]

New Wine, New Wineskins

In the June 1906 interview with the *Courier-Journal*, Holcombe stated that the traditional strategies of rescue mission work were no longer yielding a sufficient harvest of redeemed souls and reformed lives. Rather, many vagrants simply partook of the generosity of the Mission without any aspirations toward moral transformation or social mobility. Charity for society's underserved and destitute gave way to concern that the Mission was actually encouraging a conglomeration of tramps who had little aspirations toward spiritual or social improvement. This realization changed Holcombe's approach to such a degree that he was no longer able to invest himself in the lives of the men who visited the facility. He conceded that the Mission needed a fresh approach, one which made investment in children its primary focus:

> "For the last few years, I have not fed or clothed a single tramp. I feel that the age of that sort of charity is over, and that we should turn our attention to another field of charity that is just beginning to open up. I don't think that we

have made many converts among the class of people with whom we have been dealing in the last few years. We are not to start on a new field. We are going to start on the children, and when they grow up there will be no occasion for a Holcombe Mission of the old type."[3]

Cardwell's vision for the Union Gospel Mission included ministries designed to aid and influence children toward education and healthy life development. Holcombe, in his remarks to the *Courier-Journal*, previewed the Cardwell-era of the Mission's work:

"Mrs. Cardwell will have under her assistants who will visit the homes of the people and bring the children to the school. We will have classes, and playrooms, and will keep them off the street, clean them, take care of them, feed them and educate them, and send them home to their parents every evening cleaned and edified inwardly and outwardly. I think that the differences between their appearances will bring home to the parents a sermon that would not have had nearly as much effect had it been delivered at a church. We will have evening classes for the parents and working children, and a Gospel meeting every night, at which attendance will be voluntary."[4]

Cardwell took over administration of the existing ministries, with the exception of the nightly preaching services which were reduced to three nights per week and conducted by various pastors and laymen. If no preacher was available, as was a frequent occurrence before the Mission employed a salaried pastor, Cardwell would share a message from the Scriptures. The attendance at the services increasingly resembled family work rather than the crowds of drunken and destitute men which had frequented the building in Holcombe's day.[5]

She aspired to take the Mission into new directions of ministry. Central to her new strategy was the establishment of a Day Nursery. The nursery staff served working mothers who needed to leave their children with caretakers on their way to work for the day.[6] In accordance with Kentucky's laws on racial segregation during the early twentieth century, the children admitted to the nursery were almost certainly exclusively white. The so-called "Day Law" came into effect in 1904 and mandated racial segregation within the same school facility or schools located less than twenty-five miles apart until being declared illegal by the United States Supreme Court's ruling on *Brown v. Board of Education* (1954).[7]

Attention was also directed upon improving the Mission's physical facilities. The building needed to be improved by public bathrooms, and the directors made plans to augment the property lot with low rent apartment houses. Holcombe hoped to see the main mansion restored to its former aesthetic glory as it had been under the ownership of Ben Smith.[8]

Cardwell recounted her memory of taking over from Holcombe as being a daunting burden, but one which she undertook in faith, trusting God would ultimately provide the means to accomplish the work:

> "Although I felt unequal to the great task set before me, I humbly and prayerfully accepted the great responsibility. Women and children were more and more claiming my attention. Three large dormitories were opened, painted, and furnished with white iron beds and other necessary equipment; also a dining-room and a kitchen were provided. A competent matron was installed. It was marvelous how evident was God's presence in all of our undertakings."[9]

Cardwell's Day Nursery served the needs of single mothers who may have themselves been transients arriving in Louisville hoping to find steady work. The nursery began in a small room adjoining Cardwell's office until a larger room in the house was fitted to accommodate more children. A gift from a Sunday School class of the Highland Presbyterian Church—taught by one of Cardwell's dearest friends—provided for the building and equipping of a bathroom for the nursery. The appeal of child care was a noble cause which inspired the support of churches and the public. Local businesses provided coal for heating the building and milk for feeding the babies.[10] In its first year of operation, the Day Nursery welcomed an attendance of over 2,500.[11] The Day Nursery became one of the Mission's most popular services and expanded in 1924 to include a school with Miss Nancy Rubel serving as its first teacher in the revised incarnation.[12]

The Industrial School had evolved into a sewing school over the years, and the service became an important means of mending donated clothing, shoes, and stockings to make them fit for distribution to needy children. During Holcombe's latter years at the Mission, a shoe cobbler had kept a shop in the building's basement, which further strengthened the ministry's ability to repair and distribute clothing across the neighborhood. Not only did the sewing school meet the needs of providing adequate clothing to the community, but it also served as a way to train children in the work of sewing.[13] An extension of the sewing school was the organization of Mother's Club meetings in 1907 which served mothers by teaching them the trade in addition to providing them meals.[14]

Under the superintendency of Cardwell, the Mission expanded its ministries, offering a medical staff in its building, although it still aimed to raise $3,000 for its annual expense, which had been a consistent fundraising goal since 1895. By 1908, the Mission was receiving about $1,600 annually through the rental of some of the rooms of its building.[15] The campus offered a daily free clinic with a physician who could respond freely to all calls for his services.[16] The physician, identified by one local newspaper clipping as Dr. S. C. Quniby, filled prescriptions, treated visitors, and occasionally performed operations.[17]

With the revival of the Mission's vitality in ministry, its Board of Managers once again resumed regular meetings and played a more active role in coordinating administrative affairs than it had under Holcombe's last ten years as superintendent. The evangelistic work was organized by one of the Mission's committees. The evangelism committee conducted open-air meetings in front of the main building which bore some fruit of conversion. Osborne, in addition to his duties as Mission president, directed the Sunday School committee for many years, securing teachers and supplies for the work. The Mission also managed the upkeep of a playground on the Mission's grounds, which had been established under Holcombe's tenure.[18]

Although the Mission's work after Holcombe proceeded in fruitful faithfulness, fundraising remained a challenge, especially with property maintenance, repairs, and mortgage payments on the building. Renting rooms in the mansion to tenants approved by the board became a necessary source of income in keeping the Mission financially stable. Whereas Holcombe's name had long been a source of financial fruit for the Mission due to his public reputation, the ministry's successors could no longer expect to reap the royalties from its connection to its famous founder.[19] Although Holcombe initially paid visits to the Mission as an honored guest during his first year of retirement, his reputation with his old ministry partners appears to have quickly soured for reasons undocumented.

THE END OF HOLCOMBE

In an unexpected turn of events, Holcombe grew restless in retirement and resolved to return to Mission work in less than two years out of the saddle. Under Cardwell, however, the Union Gospel Mission desired to proceed with its new leadership and new focus. The minutes of the Board of Directors meeting of January 8, 1908 noted that President Osborne had received a letter from Holcombe's attorney, Col. B. H. Young, threatening a lawsuit against the Mission.[20] No information was provided as to what Holcombe's complaint was against the Mission, but the minutes note that the directors instructed Osborne to confer with the Fidelity Trust Company regarding the matter. At the March 12 meeting of the directors, Osborne appointed a committee—consisting of himself and three other directors—to act in defense of the Mission against Holcombe's suit. The April 9 minutes record that Osborne reported as to the status of the suit without providing any details other than that "Attorney Woodbury would watch the proceedings." At the same meeting, the directors named a committee of two—S. S. Waltz and H. W. McGlothlin—"to draw up bylaws and rules to govern this body."[21]

On April 27, Osborne reported to the directors that Holcombe's suit against the Mission had been withdrawn—though no further details were recorded.[22] The board also commended Waltz and McGlothlin for their "faithful and efficient services rendered in drafting by-laws and rules to govern this board."[23] This revision of the Mission's constitution and by-laws required approval from delegates invited from all the evangelical churches in Louisville, and the directors requested Cardwell to call upon the churches for this purpose at the next regular meeting of the board.[24] The Mission adopted the revised constitution on June 15, 1908, although the board's minutes do not specify the nature or extent of changes made to the Mission's constitution and by-laws.[25] In the spring of 1909, the Mission board approved the printing of 2,500 – 5,000 copies for distribution of a booklet detailing the work and history of the Mission to promote public awareness and fundraising, although this publication—which may have publicized the notable constitutional changes—may now be lost to history.[26]

Having abandoned this second legal coup to take back control of the Union Gospel Mission, Holcombe dedicated himself to pursuing gospel mission work under his own name, with a focus upon evangelistic street preaching as had characterized his ministry in its earliest years. Despite his advanced age, Holcombe evidenced renewed energy for the work.[27] Newspapers reported that he even hoped to open his own day nursery.[28]

He used the "Holcombe Mission" title as a banner for his work, which resulted in obvious identity confusion for those who had so closely associated Holcombe with the institution of the Union Gospel Mission. He solicited funding from the public and old friends, thus depriving the Union Gospel Mission of the support of such persons who were still drawn to the Holcombe name. Osborne found Holcombe's establishment of alternative rescue missions to be adversarial to the sustained work of the Union Gospel Mission, noting in a 1912 address that "the Superintendent who retired greatly in debt to the Mission antagonized its work with rival missions and has for years solicited contributions from the public."[29] Over the next few years, the Union Gospel Mission struggled under mounting debt and a shortage of funding due to competition from other gospel mission ministries such as Holcombe's personal endeavors.[30]

In his last years of life, Holcombe made several attempts at establishing a stable rescue mission in Louisville; one such endeavor was located on Brook Street and another was located on Green Street. All of his attempts failed in a matter of months. Holcombe also divided his attention between caring for his sick wife—until her death on May 22, 1912—and trying desperately to acquire sufficient funding to continue his passion for mission work. However, none of his financial strategies—which included digging oil wells on his Elizabethtown farm—bore the fruit he desired. One of his last ill-fated attempts was the opening of a store on Louisville's Second Street selling a tonic marketed as a potent medical cure-all. Holcombe's earthly treasures depleted in his last years leaving him with only "the work of spreading the gospel" as his driving life purpose. Widowed and suffering from rapidly declining health, Holcombe sold his farm and took residence with his daughter Pearl's family.[31]

Despite the turbulent relationship between Holcombe and the Union Gospel Mission, he still loved the institution, and his last wish was to die in the Mission's mansion. Cardwell honored her old mentor's request, allowing the frail and cancer-stricken Holcombe to return to the facility to live out his last days at the place where he had dedicated his life's work. After about a month of sick-bed residency at the Mission, Holcombe died on February 24, 1916 in the care of his daughter Mayme.[32] The funeral service for Holcombe was also hosted at the Mission the following Saturday, and his remains were buried in Elizabethtown, with the Union Gospel Mission directors—including Osborne—serving as honorary pallbearers.[33]

Osborne's own tenure on the Mission's board ended abruptly on June 11, 1917 after W. E. Pilcher, an Episcopalian and a premiere pipe organ businessman, was elected to succeed him as president. The minutes record that after the reading of the Nominating Committee's recommendation report, "President Thos. D. Osborne retired from the meeting without any explanation, whereupon the Vice President Rev. W. N. Briney, took charge of the meeting."[34] Cardwell wrote Osborne a week later expressing her appreciation for him and expressing her hope that he would continue his work with the Sunday School ministry.[35] Pilcher and the rest of the board members also hoped Osborne would continue with the Mission in the office of vice-president, but he declined; C. O. Ewing—of Ewing & Sons Creamery—ultimately filled the vacated vice-president position.

FOUNTS OF MANY BLESSINGS

The Union Gospel Mission needed to continue payments on its mortgage in addition to making improvements to the existing facilities to better serve the expanded work directed toward women and children. At the Mission board's annual meeting in 1916, Cardwell proposed the addition of enlarged quarters on the building's third floor and the installation of a laundry room in the basement.[36] Throughout her tenure, Cardwell employed a circle of women who assisted her at the Mission, each having particular oversight of the various departments such as the Day Nursery and the office. They received modest monthly salaries and most boarded within the building with laundry services provided.[37]

Mrs. Elizabeth Robinson, who had trained at the Moody Bible Institute in Chicago, became Cardwell's assistant in 1916—at a salary of $15 per month—paying special attention to the Mother's Club. Robinson served as assistant superintendent for sixteen years until her death in 1931, in addition to helping with secretarial and bookkeeping work. She taught a Sunday School class in a "tender but very firm" manner and earned the love of the children and Cardwell's highest trust.[38] In 1917, Cardwell assigned Robinson the special assignment of soliciting funding for the Mission in addition to her regular duties. With the approval of the Mission's board, Robinson received authorization to solicit funds two days a week and to be compensated an extra $10 a month for her efforts.[39]

In October of 1917, the Mission took a monumental step in securing a steady source of funding for its various ministries and services, as the managing board decided to join the Louisville Federation of Social Agencies—the organization known today as Metro United Way—which came into existence the same year in response to the city's growing need for community planning and fund-raising for the efficient coordination of social services.[40] The Union Gospel Mission was one of twenty-five charter agencies of the LFSA.[41]

Membership in the Federation became a bulwark for stabilizing the Mission's financial standing. By June 10 of the following year, the Mission had received $1,267.33 in funding from the Federation, amounting to nearly 36% of its total annual income.[42] Previously, the Mission was entirely dependent upon donations and rent collected from the tenants of its facilities. Now, with the backing of the Federation, the Mission was no longer at the mercy of private donations but had a steady source of funding which would become its lifeline over the next two decades.

The Union Gospel Mission continued to establish itself as a leader in the city's social services. In 1917, the Mission opened a boarding home for homeless young girls who had been dismissed by orphanages or placed by the Juvenile Court. The Mission used a secondary house, located at 102 East Jefferson Street, for this purpose, which Cardwell furnished with décor, books, and musical instruments. Cardwell worked the Mission during the day and slept with the girls in the boarding home at night. Cardwell, along with a board of all-women managers, worked to secure employment for the girls in department stores, switch-board operations, and factories. A portion of the money earned by the girls at these places of employment went toward their boarding fee. Cardwell also arranged for some of the girls to receive education at the Ahrens Trade School and the Young Women's Christian Association.[43]

In the Mission's second year of association with the Louisville Federation of Social Agencies, it received over $3,500 in social service funding, amounting to nearly 60% of its annual income. This substantial increase in funding allowed the Mission to devote more budgetary resources to property maintenance and staff salaries for committed workers such as Robinson.[44] Funding from the Federation continued to increase in successive years, supplanting rent and fundraising as the primary supporter of the Mission's expenses.

In 1920, the Mission received an additional bonus of a $5,000 bequest from the late John R. Gheens, the prominent Kentucky businessman behind the Gheens & Brother wholesale grocery company. The legal terms of the Gheens bequest became the subject of some confusion before the Mission received the money because Gheens had designated the money for "the Steve Holcomb [*sic*] Mission." On account of Holcombe's splits with the Union Gospel Mission and his attempts to start new rescue missions using his own name, there was no longer any organization in Louisville using the "Holcombe Mission" moniker in 1920.

The difficult task of sorting out the financial arrangement fell to John's nephew Charles Edwin Gheens, a devout Baptist and the heir to the family's empire. He did not consider the Union Gospel Mission to be the intended beneficiary of his uncle's bequest, and he scoured through the bound volume of the Union Gospel Mission's minute book looking to find evidence supporting his argument.[45] Ultimately, C. E. Gheens found the record book too unorganized to make any definitive conclusion on the matter, so he offered to let the board of the Union Gospel Mission make the final good-faith decision. He sent the Mission a check along with a letter explaining his position, allowing its board members to determine whether or not to claim the compensation. The Union Gospel Mission claimed the money without hesitation and invested the money into a Gheens Fund to reserve for special ministry needs.[46]

The Great Depression

The Louisville Federation of Social Agencies underwent a series of name changes throughout its early years, changing first to the Welfare League in 1919 and again the Louisville Community Chest in 1923. By 1923, the organization was able to raise well over a half million dollars for charitable causes, of which the Union Gospel Mission was an annual beneficiary.[47] By 1927, the Mission received in excess of $10,000 annually from the Community Chest.[48] At the onset of America's Great Depression, however, the Mission's budget began to be gradually reduced by the Community Chest, as the organization became stricter with its disbursement criteria, being unable to reach its own yearly fundraising goals. Consequently, salaries of the Mission's employees had to be reduced by the end of 1931.[49]

Elizabeth Robinson, Mission assistant superintendent and bookkeeper, died suddenly on October 16, 1931. Cardwell, given her advancing age, was desperate for someone who had previously worked alongside her and would be fully qualified as her potential successor. After the loss of Robinson, Cardwell called upon the services of Mrs. Maude Melton Abner, who had previously assisted the Mission as Cardwell's office secretary from 1907 to 1910. Abner recalled Cardwell's plea to her over a phone call the morning after Robinson's death: "If you will come and be my Assistant Superintendent I will be able to continue the work, because it is impossible for me now to train another worker."[50]

Abner converted to Christianity as a young child and formed her core religious convictions from involvement with a Baptist church. By the time she returned to the Mission in 1931, she had already invested a lifetime in the cause of Southern Baptist home missions and administrative work. She graduated from the Woman's Missionary Union Training School—which held classes on the campus of The Southern Baptist Theological Seminary—in 1912, served as the office secretary to the great Baptist preacher M. E. Dodd, and spent nearly two decades in service in various Baptist causes in Kentucky, Louisiana, and Oklahoma.[51]

Cardwell resigned her position of Mission superintendent at the end of 1932, recommending that Abner fill the vacancy. The Mission's board voted to retain Cardwell under the title of Superintendent Emeritus "on account of her splendid work and long term of service, that she be continued a member of this Mission, as well as spiritual advisor and representative, and that she retain her residence at the Mission."[52] Cardwell also took residence within one of the rooms of the Mission's mansion, whereas she had previously resided in the Mission's boarding home for girls.[53]

The Mission board formally approved Abner as Cardwell's successor in the position of superintendent on March 10, 1933. At the same meeting, Pilcher read a request from the Community Chest that the Mission discontinue its boarding home as another casualty of the Great Depression.[54] The Mission's 1934 Community Chest dwindled to only $6,579.16, and an even tougher blow came in the form of a 1933 report by the Family and Child Welfare Council, which concluded that the Mission ought to be discontinued. The committee believed that the care of transients could be more efficiently accomplished through the Travelers Aid and the Salvation Army while the Municipal Relief Bureau could more effectively place citizens with employment services. Furthermore, it deemed the work of the Mission's various departments to be too inter-related and the Day Nursery for white children being the only activity that was not duplicated by some other organization in Louisville. The Day Nursery alone did not benefit a sufficient number of children to justify a large annual expenditure, according to the view of the committee, which concluded, "In view of the entire set-up of the mission, it is questionable whether the expense is justified."[55]

Abner inherited a difficult situation in succeeding Cardwell at a time of great financial stress, but she was wholly committed to the labor. When the mansion's dining room floor required renovations in 1934, Abner contributed her own finances to secure the installation of a hard-wood floor covering to offset the difference in the reduced Community Chest contributions.[56] That same year, the Mission received permission from the Community Chest to implore churches for financial aid in building maintenance. After receiving the offering from the churches, repairs were made on the mansion windows, the basement was newly concreted, and roof ventilators were rebuilt.[57]

The Mission hoped to expand the services of its Day Nursery to reach more children, since that particular aspect of its work was the only service recognized as non-duplicated by the Family and Child Welfare Council's report of the previous year.[58] Attendance in the Day Nursery had declined by nearly 50% between 1930 and 1932, and the Mission needed to instill confidence of its ongoing viability with the Community Chest.[59] Nevertheless, the Community Chest once again reduced its budgetary allowance to the Mission by another thousand dollars for 1935.[60] As a result, the Mission had to reduce its Nursery, eliminating services for older children, which in turn further reduced another source of income.[61] As the Mission prepared to celebrate its Jubilee anniversary in 1935, it had fifty years of history to appreciate but faced an uncertain future.

6

FROM LAMENTATIONS
TO SERENDIPITY

At the June 14, 1935 meeting of the Mission's Board of Managers, superintendent Maude Abner commemorated the Jubilee anniversary of the organization in a paper entitled "Past, Present, Future of the Union Gospel Mission," which she distributed to churches throughout the year.[1] In addition to recounting the Mission's eventful fifty year history, Abner shared insight as to the Mission's strained financial state:

> "While we have been greatly handicapped during the depression we have done a most wonderful work. We were reduced again and again from a financial standpoint; also in workers. Much to our regret, the Girl's Boarding Home, which was a wonderful asset to the work, had to be closed … Our third floor also had to be closed against the helpless women and children and they were sent to other organizations. During 1933 we admitted 109 and discharged 102, leaving only the seven workers and helpers in the Mission."[2]

Offering a word of encouragement, Abner appealed to the Mission's spiritual core:

"All social work is marvelous, but we must begin at the fountain source to correct all evils. Christ must come into the heart before reformation or regeneration can begin. So we lay much stress on the religious side of the work."[3]

With the scaling back of the Mission's departments, attention focused upon the Sunday School, the Wednesday afternoon Mother's Club, the Sunday evening Young People's Meeting, Vacation Bible School, the three nightly preaching services, and the Day Nursery.[4] Former superintendent Elizabeth Cardwell continued to reside in the Mission's mansion and provided advisement and occasional visitation.

SERIES OF SETBACKS

The Mission's aged mansion still required extensive maintenance and repairs including a new roof, offices, painting, and sidewalks. Abner prayed daily for "an outpouring of the Holy Spirit upon the hearts of the people and the workers who are helping us, and the sinners of our community for their conviction and regeneration."[5] Abner desired to publish a booklet on the Mission with hopes of raising public awareness, but the board did not have available money to spend on the endeavor.[6] The book project was also frustrated by the objection of the Community Chest, which believed that such a book might unfairly disadvantage the annual collections for its supported social agencies.[7]

The Mission suffered another blow to morale when the board's secretary-treasurer, A. G. Renau, fell ill during the Jubilee year and died in March, 1936.[8] Soon after, Rev. W. M. McKinney, the Mission's pastor of two years, resigned his position after finishing his seminary education and accepting a pastorate in West Virginia.[9] His replacement was another seminary student, C. W. Jennings, whose brief tenure with the

Mission ended in the spring of 1937 upon his own acceptance of a church pastorate.[10]

In addition to its internal financial and staffing troubles, the Mission faced the possibility that other ministries might make its work appear irrelevant in the eyes of charitable benefactors. The Long Run Baptist Association, the missionary network of Southern Baptist churches across Jefferson County, had a desire to open a rescue mission in close proximity to the Union Gospel Mission. At the Mission board's December 12, 1936 meeting, the directors authorized its executive committee to meet with a committee from the Long Run Baptist Association to communicate its concerns. The Long Run Baptist Association's committee was headed by its chief missionary Fred C. Tucker, and Abner—who had strong Southern Baptist ties—advised him not to proceed with the endeavor since the presence of a Baptist mission might further discourage the Community Chest from supporting the Union Gospel Mission.[11] Talks of possible cooperation between the Mission and the LRBA continued.

The Mission received a sliver of hope in an otherwise grim year when the Community Chest invited its participation in their exposition to be held from January 17-21, 1937; the Mission's board members accepted the invitation and Abner reported that the Mission's booth "made a splendid showing."[12] Regardless, the Community Chest once again requested the Mission to cut its budget by more than $1,000 for the following year.[13]

Downtown Louisville itself received a harsh blow in 1937 when much of the city became partially submerged by a great flood of the Ohio River. The flood waters reached emergency levels on January 21, the last night of the Community Chest's exhibition. As the volunteers scurried to disassemble the booths, cots were placed in the auditorium of Armory to accommodate refugees. The Mission building survived the flood waters—it "stood high and dry as a lighthouse tower," in Abner's words—and temporarily housed refugees throughout the month of February who had been displaced by the disaster. Within the Mission facility, 4,000 people were inoculated against typhoid fever, and the Day Nursery provided 160 meals to refugee children.[14]

The Mission's mansion did not escape the flood without damage, however, as water seeped into the basement's furnace pit, and the janitor suffered minor injuries due to an explosion of the furnace. But the greatest injury to the Mission's spirit came in the death of mansion resident and emeritus superintendent Elizabeth Cardwell on April 7 upon suffering a heart attack on her way to a Wednesday evening prayer meeting at the Broadway Methodist Temple Church. Cardwell's funeral, like that of her mentor Steve P. Holcombe, was held at the Mission with remarks by some of its former pastors and board members.[15] Cardwell's will bequeathed the residue of her estate to the Union Gospel Mission for the specific purpose of "missionary work among the people, taking the Gospel to them in their homes, under the supervision of The Union Gospel Mission."[16]

In spite of mounting financial and personnel difficulties, the Mission received a Christmas gift in late 1937 in the form of a neon sign illuminating the expression "God is Love," which would became an iconic identifier upon the mansion's façade for decades to come.[17] At the September 10, 1937 meeting of the Mission's Board of Managers, they approved a special fund that would employ a field worker at a maximum salary of $15 per month.[18] The field work was conducted by new Mission pastor S. R. Arnold until he had to cease from the work for several months due to prolonged illness and hospital stays between Fall 1938 and Spring 1939.

Abner drew personal comfort from the words of Psalm 56:3: "What time I am afraid I will trust in the Lord." This certainty in the goodness of the Mission's work in sowing seed of eternal worth motivated her to press on throughout the external and internal difficulties of the Mission. The Vacation Bible School ministry of 1938 saw thirty-three conversions, in spite of the illness of pastor Arnold. She wrote that: "There were constant rumblings in the distance of an oncoming storm but all we could do was to wait, pray, trust and continue with our work."[19]

In 1938, the Salvation Army, under the chairmanship of Smith Bailey, contacted Mission president W. E. Pilcher to propose a program to subsume the entirety of the Union Gospel Mission's work and replace all staff with its own workers. The Mission's executive committee met several times with representatives from the Salvation Army to consider the feasibility of how both organizations might work cooperatively to improve the social and spiritual lives of the community, but the Mission decided on December 9 to notify the Salvation Army that the Mission would be both unwilling and unable to cease their explicitly religious work under the terms of its charter. The Mission promised to better communicate with the Salvation Army in the coordination of its yearly programs in hopes that the organizations could work more efficiently in their respective tasks.[20]

LOCKED OUT OF THE CHEST

Throughout the 1930s, the Community Chest had steadily decreased its funding of the Union Gospel Mission each year. Despite the best efforts of Abner and the Mission's board to adjust the budgets and accommodate all requests of the social service agency, the Mission lost its funding completely in 1939. Roy Sorenson, the chairman of the Chest's Survey Committee, attended the Mission's board meeting of March 31 to explain the reason for dropping the organization from its supported agencies "had nothing to do with the religious work" but that the extent of the Mission's social activities no longer justified the amount of budget expended.[21]

With the Community Chest funding scheduled to cease at the end of 1939, the Mission now faced the dilemma of how to proceed with its business in 1940 and, if possible, beyond. The Mission faced two undesirable alternatives: one being to abandon the facilities and turn over the work to another organization (evangelical churches or a social service) and the other being to carry on the work in hopes of obtaining funding from interested laymen.[22] Abner remained adamant that the Mission must not separate its religious work from its social services, even if that meant resignation to the fact it would never again reclaim its status as an agency of the Community Chest.

Abner boldly encouraged the executive committee to continue the work in faith, making as many painful sacrifices necessary to stay within a budget reduced by nearly $7,000. One option would be to dissolve the position of Mission pastor and recruit volunteer preachers and seminary students to provide services without charge. In addition to staff-wide pay reductions, Abner herself volunteered to work a year without pay.[23]

Despite the willingness of Abner and her staff to sacrifice financially for the sake of the Mission, the signature of the Fair Labor Standards Act of 1938 by United States President Franklin D. Roosevelt made it difficult for the Mission to comply with new federal standards for minimum wages and maximum hourly workweeks.[24] Abner submitted a ten-month budget proposal to the Mission's board on June 22, whereby the reminder of the Gheens and Special funds would support the basic expenses of the Mission and its salaries until exhaustion, and a pastor/field visitor position would be funded by the Cardwell fund. The Mission would then appeal to churches and individuals to take greater interest in its work and "definitely trust our Heavenly Father to make our funds reach as far as possible and to look to Him to supply our needs as He has promised in Philippians 4:19: 'But my God shall supply ALL your need according to His riches in glory by Christ Jesus.'"[25]

HARD, HONEST CONVERSATIONS[26]

With the Mission having been cut off from social service funding, Abner sought to refocus upon its fundamental purpose, as outlined in its charter to "preach the Gospel to these wicked and abandoned men, women, and children."[27] A Special Program Planning Committee assembled on the afternoon of July 17 to consider all feasible plans for continuance of the Mission; this committee consisted of five members of the board: W. E. Pilcher, Judge J. T. O'Neal, Dr. John Lowe Fort, William Herrman (committee chairman), and Walter Distelhorst. The record of their meeting listed four options: (1) proceed under the plan previously suggested by Mrs. Abner on June 22, (2) proceed under Salvation Army auspices, (3) proceed under the management of some qualified workers, man and wife, or (4) quit.[28]

Fort spoke bluntly about the declining relevance of the Mission's religious and social ministries, noting that religious meetings rarely featured attendance beyond staff and that the continuance of a day nursery might not be the best use of the building's resources. Furthermore, because more mothers were working in their homes (Fort's assumption) and the Broadway Baptist Church (then located at the intersection of Brook and Broadway about three blocks south of the Mission) operated its own nursery supported by the Works Progress Administration, Fort viewed the Mission's efforts in this area as an unnecessary redundancy of efforts bearing little fruit; the Mission should focus all its resources on recruiting dynamic preachers and bigger meetings that could attract large crowds. To this end, he recommended the services of Mr. and Mrs. Bob Herndon to take over administrative duties of the Mission—the husband was a Baptist preacher who also served in the Juvenile Court and the wife had social work experience—at a joint annual salary of $2,400 and board. Fort believed that Herndon had the influence and charisma to present successfully the Mission's cause to the churches as well as network with the financially affluent citizens of Louisville.[29]

Pilcher still held hope that the Mission might be able to develop a program that could win back the support of the Community Chest, but O'Neal admonished the committee that there was no wisdom in looking back, and if the Mission could not inspire the evangelical churches of the city to support their expenses past 1939, then there was no point in continuing the course.[30] O'Neal—as Abner had already done in earlier statements—expressed his conviction that all funds and facilities should be used for the purposes intended by its founders, namely that "the Mission was established to preach the gospel and save souls."[31] The committee's discussion closed without any unanimous consensus on a course of action, save for the desire to hear from Abner regarding her outline for a definite program of work for the Mission's remaining year.

Abner wrote to Herrman expressing her disapproval with the committee's consideration of the two proposals: absolving its work under the auspices of the Salvation Army and hiring a man and wife team of "qualified workers" to manage the work. Abner took offense at the notion, noting her own credentials as a graduate of the Baptist W.M.U. Training School and twenty-seven years of social service work experience, among many other career accomplishments. She asserted that the Mission, in its present state, did not necessitate the employment of a male superintendent since the charter plainly stated that the Mission's work ought to be to "give the gospel to wicked and abandoned men, women, and children," and although many institutions of the city attended to the needs of men, no other place in the city cared for women and children in the degree that the Mission did. If the Mission should turn over its day nursery to the authority of W.P.A., then "we are proving untrue to the trust that has been placed in us by the churches of the city and untrue to God." Abner believed that no other institution in Louisville could offer the same degree of care or hourly availability for needy children and their working parents than the Mission's day nursery.

Abner disputed Fort's assumption that most mothers worked at home, as her experience in the field testified that most mothers worked in laundries, factories, restaurants, and stores. If the committee did not consider either herself or Elizabeth Cardwell sufficiently capable of handling drunken men, how could they consider any man capable enough to handle drunken women? She feared that many men might model harmful habits (notably smoking cigarettes and drinking) around the children, which the Mission staff taught the children to avoid. Abner even dared to challenge the moral fitness of Fort's preferred man for the work of ministry with children, stating:

> "I am not absolutely positive but it seems to me that I remember seeing Mr. Herndon in the Community Chest meetings smoking cigarettes with the other workers around his table with both men and women."[32]

In her estimation, the Mission owed its best efforts to persevere until the last dollar in its treasury, as anything less than that would amount to unfaithfulness to God, its supporters, and its previous superintendents Holcombe and Cardwell. Thus, "quitting" was no a viable option from her point of view, as "God's condemnation would be upon us." Abner urged the committee to adopt her suggested budget, in addition to continually seeking funding from the churches in faith that God would provide guidance.

On the morning of August 22, the Mission's program committee met again to hear the proposal of the Salvation Army's W. W. Bourterse, who recognized the Mission's strategic location for good in a needy neighborhood. Under the Salvation Army's oversight, the Mission could maintain its charter, property, and Board of Managers; though the Army would install a married couple to oversee the daily affairs, many of which would remain the same as the Mission had previously offered. The Mission committee also interviewed Bob Herndon and his wife, who proposed their own suggested program and budget. The Herndons estimated that $7,500 would be necessary to operate their suggested annual program at the Mission, with 72% of funds being dedicated toward salaries for six staff.[33]

ABNER'S LAST STAND

On October 24, the Program Planning Committee met to propose a $5,037 budget and plan of operation for 1940; S. R. Arnold would be employed for the first four months of the year at a salary of $60 per month supported by the Cardwell Fund.[34] At its November 10 meeting, the Mission Board of Managers voted to accept the committee's recommended program and to revise the Mission's constitution in order to allow for an enlarged board of managers "in order to bring responsibility to the churches in a larger measure for the Mission's continuance."[35] Abner bestowed a $1,000 donation to provide the Mission with extended time to solicit the churches for funding, and the Louisville Welfare Department granted the Mission a permit to solicit donations.[36]

The Mission hosted a December 5 luncheon at the Kentucky Hotel in order to present their financial needs to representatives of various evangelical churches of the city.[37] Only a small number of guests accepted the invitation and the endeavor did not prove successful. Abner wrote that "it was fortunate that at this time we were buried in the work of Christmas for the children so we could not dwell on any disappointments."[38] Two of the Mission's board members, O'Neal and Harold W. Tribble—both of the Baptist persuasion, resigned their seats at the end of 1939.

The Mission saw increased attendance in its chapel services in January, 1940. It began serving sandwiches and bread loaves at the Tuesday and Thursday evening meetings, as it no longer had to abide by the Community Chest's prohibition against distributing refreshments. Local bakeries and other businesses donated bread and materials for making sandwiches.[39] Rev. S. A. Arnold resigned as pastor at end of February as his graduation from The Southern Baptist Theological Seminary neared; the Mission did not hire a replacement but simply called upon pastors from churches across the denominational spectrum to provide services.[40]

Despite the Mission Board of Managers' wishes to enlarge its membership, its leadership suffered depletion when Fort died in April. The Executive Committee met on May 17 to elect replacement members and review the Mission's financial situation, concluding it was an "apparent impossibility" that the Mission would be able to raise enough money to meet an annual budget of $7,000 and that the present program of the Mission must soon cease. The Committee recommended "that the Board seek to interest other religious organizations either independent or an agency of the Community Chest who would be financially able to carry forward the important work that has been so ably developed by Mrs. Abner and her staff."[41] The Committee commended Abner for her labor, and recommended that her donation of $1,000 be returned to her if and when the Mission should be discontinued.

Pilcher informed Abner that the Mission work would be impossible to continue, but the latter continued to trust that God might provide a means for the work to continue even as she mourned for the looming dismissal of her co-workers and the children of her

Day Nursery. She dedicated hours to prayer and meditation upon Lamentations 2:19: "Arise, cry out in the night: in the beginning of the watches pour out thine heart like water before the face of the LORD: lift up thy hands toward him for the life of thy young children that faint for hunger in the top of every street."[42]

At the June 7 meeting of the Board of Managers, Abner offered a desperate proposal for the Mission to permit her to fund the entire endeavor at her own personal expense for the year of 1941:

> "My purpose will be to run the Mission on faith in God and His promises and to render a monthly account to a Board who will be willing to walk with Him by faith to carry on this work. My purpose will also be, not to lower the standard of the Mission by becoming a beggar, but to tell Him our needs who is able to help more abundantly than any of us can ask or think, and to bring the Mission on a higher basis than it is now."[43]

The board decided to grant Abner this request for the limit of one month, after which the matter would be reassessed for future consideration. In spite of all the ominous signs of the Mission's demise, it still had much work to be done that summer. Abner and her staff proceeded to throw every effort into the Mission's Vacation Bible School, which saw an enrollment of two hundred children and eight professions of faith.[44] The Oscar Ewing & Sons Creamery provided milk for the school free of charge.[45]

As Abner reflected upon the Mission's seemingly bleak future, she reconsidered the Long Run Baptist Association's interest in opening a denominational mission in the Haymarket neighborhood. In 1936, Abner had pleaded with the Association's missionary Fred Tucker not to open a Baptist mission near the vicinity of the Union Gospel Mission. In 1940, she realized that the Southern Baptists were the single denomination best suited to continue mission work in the Mission's Jefferson Street property. Abner received permission from Pilcher to contact the Long Run Association to inquire if it would consider the Mission's facilities as a place to conduct its own services.

The Mission and the Long Run Association had a common member, H. Cornell Goerner, who also served as professor of missions at The Southern Baptist Theological Seminary from 1938 to 1957. Goerner, who had been elected to the Mission's board on May 10, served as Long Run representative at the July 5 board meeting. He presented a tentative program of social and religious work desired by the Long Run Association for the community surrounding the Union Gospel Mission. Goerner reported that the Long Run Association welcomed an audience with the Union Gospel Mission's board to discuss plans to incorporate the plan. The board received Goerner's report with enthusiasm, and Abner withdrew her June 14 proposition to self-support the Mission in light of positive new developments.[46]

The Union Gospel Mission had endured a difficult decade of incessantly discouraging setbacks. Because of the steadfastness of Abner and others, many lives were saved and souls prepared for eternity. The passion and faith of its superintendent, staff, and board allowed it to press on through uncertain times. Now, Southern Baptists provided a sunbeam of hope to break through the dark clouds which had long encompassed the Mission.

7

THE BAPTISTS' MISSION

After the Mission's board meeting of July 5, 1940, plans moved rapidly to arrange for the installation of the Long Run Baptist Association into the its Jefferson Street building on 114 East Jefferson Street. Southern Seminary professor H. Cornell Goerner had presented a tentative program of work on behalf of the Association that would include mission services, supervised recreational activity, a library, and daily religious activities such as Vacation Bible School and after-school services for children. Furthermore, the proposal also suggested the organization of a Baptist church within the Mission's building, and the employment of a male superintendent/pastor, a director of Religious Education, a property manager, and volunteer workers with a cumulative salary estimation of $2,700. Sources of income would be split equally between the Long Run Association's board and Louisville churches, while also supplemented by individual donors.[1]

One month later, the Mission's executive committee and Maude Abner, superintendent, met with three members of the Long Run's Missionary Committee: Dr. E. C. Stevens, Dr. E. F. Estes, and Mrs. W. H. McKeigan. Stevens, the committee chairman, informed the Mission board that the Long Run desired to have charge of the Mission for a one-year preliminary period after which time a decision could be made on the sale of the building and property, with the Association given the privilege of first refusal to purchase. During this first year, the Association would be responsible for all expenses with the exception that the Mission's board would function as a landlord on the property responsible for reasonable maintenance of the premises and insurance.[2] The Mission's board approved the Association's proposal in its October 8 meeting.[3]

A necessary act of business for the Mission's board was the revision of its constitution to allow Southern Baptists to take control of its work. Since its inception in 1885, the Mission's constitution had required that "the management and teaching shall be strictly evangelical and absolutely non-denominational." The board eliminated the words "and absolutely non-denominational" in its December 13 meeting. The board voted that $130 be provided to Mission employees who endured salary reductions over the course of 1940 to meet the minimum wage law; the board also authorized $200 to be reimbursed to Abner herself, if sufficient resources in the treasurer allowed once all expenses had been paid.[4]

Under the new agreement between the Union Gospel Mission and the Long Run Baptist Association, Abner would finish her tenure as superintendent throughout the month of January, 1941 in order to close the Mission's accounts, audit the books, and file the records. After completing her service, Abner joined the Mission's Board of Directors who continued to meet occasionally throughout the year for updates on the transition. The name of the institution initially remained "Union Gospel Mission" under the operation of the Long Run Baptist Association.[5]

Abner delivered her final superintendent's report to the Mission directors on January 17, 1941. After summarizing the Mission's progress from the previous year, she shared her sentiments on the transition, which though perhaps bittersweet were optimistic for the future:

> "I regret that it is necessary for our work as Union Gospel Mission to pass into the hands of another, but at the same time I am greatly rejoiced that it is being taken over by the Long Run Baptist Association, and I now say, as I said to Dr. H. C. Goerner in August, that it would be impossible for me to be Superintendent and that they need not consider me at all for I believe it is the Lord's will for me to take a rest at this time, for I feel that the time has come that I must either give up the work or give up my life of usefulness later on. May I say the nine years and four months of my labors under the Union Gospel Mission Board has been a pleasure, and I thank each of you for all of your consideration and courtesy extended to me over these years. I prize your confidence in me. May Heaven's blessings abide upon each of you and your families and the work and the Long Run Baptist Association, and all who have come and gone from the beloved Union Gospel Mission."[6]

Planting a Baptist Mission

General charge over the Mission was entrusted to Clarence L. Jordan, the Long Run Association's Superintendent of Missions. Jordan had earned two degrees from The Southern Baptist Theological Seminary between 1933 and 1939, but his most influential ministry opportunities in Louisville came through his involvement in the Long Run Baptist Association. Working primarily in the city's West End, Jordan had ministered in a dangerous and impoverished context beyond the gaze from most white Americans. While there he developed rapports with various African-American churches.[7] Jordan had received a promotion to the Association's full-time superintendent of city missions in 1940. This position took him out of the immediate context of the inner city, which was the cause of some personal disappointment as it limited his opportunities for Christian fellowship with African-American brothers and sisters.[8] Under Kentucky's Day Law, the Association's city mission work was generally segregated between the Baptist Fellowship Center at 1023 West Madison Street, which worked with African-Americans, and the Union Gospel Mission at 114 East Jefferson Street. One exception, however, appears to have been the Vacation Bible Schools, which the 1941 associational annual states were available "for white and colored," with the white children meeting in the Mission and the African-American children meeting in a separate facility across Liberty Street.[9]

As Jordan searched for a new pastor-superintendent, the Long Run Association's committee on the Mission secured the services of Miss Asenath Brewster to assume duties as the Mission's educational director in January, 1941. Brewster—who traced her ancestry back to pilgrim colonist and preacher William Brewster—had an extensive background of religious work with the General Baptists but was a founding member of the Baxter Avenue mission of the Highland Baptist Church, which identified as Southern Baptist. Before leaving the Baxter mission in 1941, Brewster had taught Sunday School for neighborhood children and worked alongside future Southern Seminary professor Frank Stagg.[10] Assisting Brewster were Helen Mellichamp, who had charge of the Day Nursery, and Marjorie Best, who worked the office and paid home visits.[11] Brewster took residence in the Mission after Abner vacated upon completing her administrative duties at the end of January.

Under the Long Run Association, the Mission program of work continued in much the same fashion as it had under the previous administration. The Association continued to operate a day nursery for children of employed mothers, the half-acre playground, classes for children and adults, sewing and housekeeping clubs, visitation of neighborhood homes, evening chapel services multiple nights a week, youth activities, Sunday School, and a Vacation Bible School.[12]

Jordan ultimately recruited to the Mission pastorate Henlee Hulix Barnette, a future Baptist ethicist who was then training at The Southern Baptist Theological Seminary.[13] Barnette first encountered Jordan after the latter spoke at a 1941 seminary chapel service, and Barnette recalled the powerful impression Jordan's words left upon him:

> "A tall, handsome, magnetic person with a gentle South Georgia drawl, [Jordan] graphically described the deplorable situation in the ghettoes of that city of Louisville. His portrayal of the famous (or infamous) Haymarket District intrigued me and the challenge he trust upon us captivated me. 'If there is a student in this chapel who isn't looking for the First Baptist Church of Podunk Hollow,' he said, 'there is a ministry for you in this city's Haymarket district where 10,000 people are unchurched.' "[14]

Even before his election as Mission pastor on September 1, Barnette began conducting prayer meetings at the Mission's chapel on Wednesday nights, and he discovered the state of the Haymarket district to be as bad as Jordan had described. Barnette spent portions of a five-year span (1941 – 1945) working at the Mission and described the neighborhood surrounding the property's First and Jefferson location as consisting of "ninety whiskey stores, bars, 'honkey tonks,' nightclubs, gambling dens, porno shops, and houses of prostitution all within a radius of three blocks."[15] Crime reports from that part of town were a constant source of headlines for the *Courier-Journal*.[16]

Barnette and Brewster worked closely together at the Mission and experienced great success in recruiting volunteer workers, most of them students at Southern Seminary. Through these arrangements, Barnette even met the student who became his wife. Students from the seminary and Woman's Missionary Union Training School also began to attend the Mission's church services, and the Association facilitated an agreement whereby Mission converts could become members of the Broadway Baptist Church while continuing to worship at the Mission facility.[17]

At the annual meeting of the Long Run Association on September 25, 1941, Brewster suggested Baptist churches better acquaint themselves with the struggles of the Haymarket district by visiting and befriending individual families; Sunday School classes could also help by securing the names and addresses of shut-ins in the vicinity of the Mission. At the same meeting, Jordan encouraged the messengers with the work of the newly organized Boy Scout troop under the volunteer leadership of seminary students; exhorting, "In the midst of vileness, crime, and immorality, there is gold and some of it has been found."[18]

Between January and September of 1941, the Long Run Association invested over $2,500 in ministries at the Union Gospel Mission.[19] The Mission's board continued to pay for only the basic facility operational expenses such as plumbing and insurance during 1941.[20] In September, the Mission's representatives met with Jordan, Brewster, and other Long Run representatives to renew another one-year contract for 1942.[21]

Pilcher, who still held the title of Mission president, was especially pleased with the Baptist stewardship of the work. The children's ministry was especially close to his heart, as he had faithfully delivered nearly one hundred Christmas stockings stuffed with gifts for around twenty-five years. He continued to make personal visits to the Day Nursery, and came to the conclusion that the Baptists had earned the right to continue the work of the Mission:

> "These people are doing a splendid work. We cannot interest the churches of the various denominations enough for them to make it possible for us to support the work. Why not give the property and contents to the Long Run Association of Baptists?"[22]

The Long Run Association had proven itself perfectly capable of supporting the Mission, and the Mission's Board of Managers met at Abner's apartment on the evening of June 1, 1942 to approve a legal disposition of the Mission property to the Association.[23] Pilcher wrote Jordan to inform him of the decision:

> "It was the unanimously expressed opinion that the Mission work now being carried on under the direction of the Long Run Baptist Association is to be commended and seems to meet the needs of the neighborhood for religious and social work. It is, therefore, the desire of the Union Gospel Mission Board to deed the Mission property, real estate, building and equipment to the Long Run Baptist Association, on condition that the said Association will continue to support and use the property for religious mission work along Evangelical lines as was intended by the founders of the Mission."[24]

The Long Run's executive board, in turn, voted to accept the Mission managers' offer on June 19.[25] At the 1942 annual meeting of the Long Run Association, Jordan cheerfully reported on the denomination's expanded control over the Mission:

"This has been a year of multiplied blessings from the Lord. He has supplied our needs and blessed our efforts with steady increases along every line. Especially do we rejoice that we are no longer 'tenants' but land-lords of the property we now occupy. During the year, the Inter-denominational Board which owned the Union Gospel Mission property, felt that the quality of our work justi-fied them in turning over to the Long Run Association all of the property and equipment belonging to the Union Gospel Mission. This was, indeed, a gracious act and it places all the more responsibility upon us to do a piece of work for the Lord that will be worthy of the faith in us."[26]

In its second year overseeing the Mission's work, the Long Run Association contributed over $5,225 to the work. Jordan praised the increased giving in allowing for the hiring of Victor Glass to work directly with boys.[27] Glass, a student at Southern Seminary, lived at the Mission with his wife.[28]

Jordan maintained involvement with the Mission through moral support, prayer meeting attendance, Sunday School teach-ing, musical ministry (he was a trumpet player), and evangelistic preaching.[29] Jordan and his wife departed from Louisville near the end of 1942 and relocated in Georgia to plant a 400-acre farm they called "Koinonia," which finally provided him the freedom to pursue his dream of fostering an interracial Christian community.[30]

THE BALL IN THE BAPTISTS' COURT

The legal transfer of the Union Gospel Mission property to the Long Run Baptist Association, was finalized in September 1943.[31] On account of the non-denominational nature of the Mission's foundational documents, due diligence required that representatives of the various cooperating denominations express their compliance with the proposal of the Mission's Board of Directors. In order to expedite the process, each of the evangelical denominations which held influence in the Mission selected a single representative to decide upon the property transfer proposal.[32]

Since joining with the Community Chest in 1917 as its primary source of funding, the Mission's ties with the evangelical churches of Louisville had grown increasingly loose, and no denomination besides the Southern Baptists showed great interest in sustaining the Mission financially. A recommendation submitted by Methodist pastor Roy H. Short revealed that most of his fellow churchmen had little, if any, direct interest in the Mission's affairs, but they wished the Baptists well in taking over the work:

> "While those who began this work, as I understand, happened to be Methodists, the Methodist Church as a church has taken little interest in the project for some years. Only a few have supported the work. I doubt that very many Methodists in the city know that they have any interest in it. . . . Now that the Mission had been dropped by the Chest, to rebuild a supporting constituency would be a task indeed. If the Baptists are willing to take over and carry on some mission work in this area I see no reason not to turn over what rights we may have. Someone ought to be doing work in this area, and if the other denominations won't and the Baptists will, I say 'God bless them in their work.' "[33]

A formal ceremony commemorating the transfer took place at the Mission on September 23, 1943, presided over by H. C. Goerner with special music and addresses delivered by Abner, Brewster,

Pilcher, Barnette, and A. W. Walker, president of the Long Run Baptist Association.[34] To quote Barnette, "The ball now was in the Baptists' court."[35] The value of the property in 1943 was estimated between $45,000 and $75,000, and the Mission's board also provided insurance policies on said property valued at $12,000 with premiums paid for three years.[36]

The Union Gospel Mission transferred the remainder of the Cardwell fund to the Methodist Mission Board of Church Extension (in accordance with the terms of Cardwell's will) and dissolved its board of directors on July 13, 1944 after settling all the cash settlements in its accounts.[37] The Mission's board also gifted Abner with $300 toward the publication of her book, *The Story of the Union Gospel Mission, 1886-1944*, in which she preserved the historical memory of the institution.[38] The Long Run Baptist Association received a supply of the books from Abner for distribution to churches at a price of $1 per copy.[39]

With the official transfer of the property, Southern Baptists inherited the full responsibilities for the upkeep of the facility. Property maintenance became an ongoing preoccupation for the Association, as the aged mansion had already seen a century of sustained usage on Jefferson Street. Even before the completion of the property transfer, there was apparent tension over defining what maintenance needs were the responsibility of the landlord (the Mission's board) and the tenant (the Association's employees). Barnette recalled that in the early years of his pastorate, "appeals to both the Protestant Board and the Baptist Board for repairs went unanswered. Each declared the other body responsible for the matter."[40]

Southern Baptists were more than equal to the task; in the early 1940s, the Long Run Association designated the most ambitious budgets in its entire history.[41] The Association made the Union Gospel Mission its highest financial priority, distributing over $7,000 for the 1942-1943 fiscal year, which amounted to nearly 53% of its annual missions budget.[42] That same year, the Mission recorded 47 baptisms and a total membership of 73 persons and an average Sunday School attendance of 114.[43] The following year, Barnette reported the Mission was reaching 35,000 people annually, and received nearly $3,000 in offerings from its own membership.[44]

The original staff appointed by the Association gradually transitioned out of the Mission into new fields of service. In 1943, Brewster moved to the Long Run's Department of Church Aid and Extension, while the Glass family relocated to the Baptist Fellowship Center.[45] Barnette and his wife finally departed the Mission in the fall of 1945, as he neared completion of his post-graduate work at Southern Seminary.[46]

BAPTIZING THE MISSION

The Long Run Association officially changed the Union Gospel Mission's name to the Central Baptist Mission in 1945, signifying that the Mission was now a thoroughly denominational endeavor. By the end of Barnette's tenure as Mission superintendent, the nature of its work very closely resembled the culture of a mid-twentieth-century Southern Baptist church, with the continuation of the day nursery six days a week. True to the spirit of Holcombe's original vision for the Mission, the ministry continued to evangelize persons who were not being sufficiently reached by traditional churches do to their economic poverty and vices. Located in close proximity to saloons, gambling establishments, and other activities associated with crime and degradation, the Mission had great success in evangelistic outreach, as it averaged a ratio of one baptism per every three members of the congregation during the 1944 associational year.[47]

Barnette's successor Gordon Hunter had previously served alongside him and kept the course.[48] Under sponsorship of the

Broadway Baptist Church, the Mission's membership had grown to around 120 persons with a total Sunday School enrollment more than 200 persons. After about a year over the Mission, Hunter vacated the position in favor of overseeing the Long Run Association's Kentucky Boys' Estate. Sherman E. Towell began his tenure as Mission pastor/superintendent, in addition to possessing broader duties of directing the Association's entire program of downtown missions. The Mission generally kept a staff of less than ten employed workers, and dozens of volunteers assisted from Baptist churches and the Southern Seminary campus.[49]

During the 1950s, the Mission made use of every available means to communicate its message. It held week-day open-air evangelistic services in the Mission's yard during the summer months, and a public address system allowed for the preaching to be heard by neighbors and citizens traveling on Jefferson Street. At each side of the street, Mission workers distributed tracts and invited passers-by to attend.[50] The Mission also expanded its outreach among children and youth, by providing safe places for fellowship. Its playground offered supervised recreation during summers, and it organized softball, basketball, and volleyball teams for boys and girls which competed in the Baptist city leagues.[51]

The Mission strategy to reach entire families often began by making an initial impact upon children. It fed families with unemployed husbands and clothed children who would have otherwise walked barefoot through the streets. The Mission's Girls Auxiliary (a Baptist missions program sponsored by the Woman's Missionary Union) prayed for the community regularly and visited shut-ins with song singing and encouragement. The weekly Mother's Club meetings created community fellowship and education within the neighborhood. Though its membership continued to grow and replenish, some of the Mission's converts elected to leave the crime-ridden Haymarket district. Anita Roper, in an article published in the Long Run Association's monthly newsletter, stated that men of the household who abandoned the pursuit of liquor were freed to invest their money on home ownership in more affluent communities:

> "At first we reach only the children, but before long the whole family is coming and is won to Christ. You say, 'Then you have some good workers.' No, they move to your communities and leave the Haymarket. Many of them buy homes when they quit spending their money on liquor. Our prayers go with them as they enter a new phase of life."[52]

Between 1949 and 1955, East Baptist Church served as the Mission's "mother church," taking over the responsibility from Broadway Baptist Church. Though the Mission had grown into a fully functional Baptist congregation in its own right, the Association did not recognize it as an independent, autonomous church since it remained an associational ministry supported by thousands of dollars each year. Newly baptized converts at the Mission became official members of the "mother church"—be it Broadway or East— but were welcomed to continue attending the Mission and serving with its own ministries.[53] The sponsoring church often provided some financial assistance to the Mission's work. Broadway Baptist reassumed the role of "mother church" in 1956.

After ten years of service as Mission superintendent, Towell resigned his post in 1956 in order to intensify his work with the Association's downtown and juvenile aid programs, and he shifted his work to the Association's recently acquired Bethel Baptist Mission.[54] Towell's successors did not have comparative longevity, as the Association appointed four men in succession to the pastorate/superintendent position between 1956 and 1961.[55]

Marvin Jackson accepted the position in 1961; although none of his three predecessors had served more than three years, Jackson broke the trend with a ten-year term. Jackson's administration proved to be one of the most eventful in the Mission's history, entailing another name change and the physical relocation of the Mission into a new campus.

NEW HOME

The Mission's mansion was deteriorating by the mid-twentieth century, in spite of the continued maintenance it had received over the decades. Some parts of the building were in such states of disrepair that it created safety concerns. The furnace had to be replaced in 1951, as the previous installation was said to have "been threatening to blow up or fall apart for several years."[56] The furnace replacement alone cost over one thousand dollars, which was partially offset through the contribution of $334 by Baptist churches and individual donors.

The Mission's advisory committee began a new building fund in 1954, which was initiated with an individual pledge of $1,000 in hopes one hundred more persons (or churches) each pledging a thousand dollars over a period of ten years.[57] By 1957, the Mission had little choice but to consider relocating their work away from its lot at 114 East Jefferson Street, as government plans for a new interstate system threatened to build an approach to the Kentucky Turnpike over the property. The Long Run Association's Executive Committee met in March to explore relocation options, including the possibility of consolidating the Mission's work with other downtown mission churches.[58]

In 1958, the Mission changed its name to Central Baptist Chapel, but continued its existing work at the same building as the Association continued to consider relocation.[59] The Mission endeavored to make financially prudent repairs to the decaying building and refocus its commitment to Christian fellowship by requesting greater commitment to worship service attendance by members and staff workers.[60]

The Louisville Urban Renewal Office contracted to purchase the Central Baptist Chapel property at 114 East Jefferson in 1962, thus officially necessitating the long-awaited campus relocation.[61] The Association's Executive Board approved a bid of $183,558.58 for the construction of a building at 733 East Jefferson Street.[62] The city demolished the historic and dilapidated Smith Mansion after the relocation of the Chapel.

In early 1963, Central Baptist Chapel made plans to merge with Faith Baptist Chapel, a mission church which had been sponsored entirely by Victory Memorial Baptist Church since 1952. Faith Chapel—located at 803 East Walnut Street—reported about 150 resident members around the time of the merger, a comparable size to the Central Chapel congregation. The two mission congregations worked together to establish a new building at the 700 block of East Jefferson Street.[63] In order to fund the new building, the Long Run Association issued an amortization of loan on the Chapel's new building for an increase more than $14,000, growing the Chapel's annual budget allocation from the Association for the 1963-64 fiscal year to nearly $34,000.[64]

With the completion of the union, a renewed downtown Baptist mission was born under the name of the Jefferson Street Baptist Chapel. The name change became official after the Long Run Association approved the recommendation of the Chapel's advisory committee in 1963.[65] Victory Memorial assumed responsibility as the Chapel's "mother church."

Louisville's urban renewal movement, which included the construction of Interstate 65, not only contributed to the physical relocation of the Jefferson Street Baptist Chapel, but also created new challenges for ministry, as many of the families of the Haymarket district found themselves displaced by the civil upheaval. Resident members of the Chapel moved their families out of the neighborhood, but regular attendance at services averaged around ninety persons during the transitional year. Chapel pastor-director Marvin Jackson called upon the Association to send volunteers to assist with weekly Bible study and youth discipleship training ministries:

> "Our emphasis is upon evangelism first, then upon every area of life. We believe that the total person is involved and that Christ makes all the difference, and when he comes into our lives there is a definite change in the whole personality. Therefore, we believe that our program here . . . must reach every age level, in fact, the entire family. . . . If you have compassion for people in a lost condition and want to help present the Gospel to them our City Mission Centers can use YOU."[66]

Cornerstone laying on the new Jefferson Street building commenced on October 20, 1963, and the Association dedicated the completed building less than seven months later on May 3, 1964.[67] Prior to the ceremonial dedication, the Chapel entered the new structure at 733 East Jefferson Street on January 26, 1964.[68] The assessed value of the new real estate exceeded $200,000 in 1964.[69]

The Jefferson Street Baptist Chapel was not content to rest upon the laurels of its new facility, as it quickly acclimated to the mission opportunities of its new community. In 1964, its Vacation Bible School enrollment was 326, with an average attendance of 170 over a two-week period. Fifty-two new members joined the fellowship, seventeen of them through profession of faith and believer's baptism. The Chapel emphasized evangelism as its primary purpose, yet it also strove to meet the physical needs of people in its mission field through the provision of food, clothing, and even the occasional emergency rent and utility bill payments for over 1,000 families.[70]

Jackson continued as JSBC director until August 1, 1971, when he resigned to accept a church pastorate.[71] Under Jackson, JSBC averaged over sixteen baptisms annually since its relocation, and its membership totaled almost 300 persons at the time of his departure. At the close of his twelve-year tenure at JSBC, Jackson recognized the changing social needs of the downtown mission, recommending to the Association the need for African-American staff members in order to more effectively reach the racially diverse community.[72] Jackson commended the continuing importance of classes in auto mechanics, wood-working, and sewing as supplementary means of meeting the needs of the community and creating opportunities for gospel presentation.[73]

After nearly thirty years under the governance and stewardship of the Long Run Baptist Association, the Mission established by Steve P. Holcombe and a Methodist church ninety-years earlier had become a thoroughly Southern Baptist endeavor in downtown Louisville. It had survived various crises of financial shortfalls, leadership turnover, name changes, and relocation. As the Jefferson Street Baptist Chapel approached its centennial anniversary, it enjoyed both a stable physical facility and the support of the Baptist denomination.

8

CHALLENGES
OF THE MODERN ERA

After the resignation of Marvin Jackson as pastor-director of the Jefferson Street Baptist Chapel, three other men held the title in succession during the 1970s.[1] During the decade, the Chapel expanded its programs of social services, receiving government funding to further its ministerial efforts. Under Jackson, the Chapel had hosted a Mother's Club course in consumer education for low income families in cooperation with Kentucky Governor Louie B. Nunn's Consumer Affairs Commission.[2] By the end of the decade, JSBC hosted a variety of government contract programs, including legal aid counseling, children's summer lunches, preventative health clinics, emergency food assistance, and senior citizen nutrition.[3]

Beginning in January 1974, JSBC participated with the Metropolitan Social Services Department to host senior adult hot lunches five days a week. The government agency paid JSBC rent for the space and also covered the costs for local catering and custodial services.[4] Most of the center's volunteer workers for serving meals came through its own congregational membership.[5] In addition, the Chapel hosted a service unit for the Metropolitan Human Resources Department in its facility.[6]

The Chapel's organizational structure increasingly resembled that of a local Baptist church, although it lacked full autonomy as an institution of the Long Run Baptist Association. During the 1971 – 1972 associational year, the Chapel's congregation elected deacons for the first time in its history. In 1975, it added programs for Boy Scouts, Cub Scouts, tutoring, and adult education.[7]

The congregation also made strides toward racial reconciliation by holding joint worship services and cooperative Vacation Bible School with the St. Paul Baptist Church, an African-American fellowship.[8] In 1975, the churches also partnered with West End Baptist Church for a racially-integrated revival. This revival was called "The Brotherhood of Man" and provided a public model of racial cooperation in religious mission for the sur-rounding community.[9]

The Chapel focused its efforts upon charitable services and evangelistic outreach to its community, with a distinctive flair. Through the organization of a "God wagon" ministry, it transported Bible teaching tools and recreational arts and crafts into a nearby housing project in small hand-decorated wagons, reaching over one hundred children a day. Taking a cue from the Union Gospel Mission's past, JSBC revitalized the weekly outdoor preaching services.[10]

FOCUS ON THE HOMELESS

In 1979, the Long Run Association's finance committee recom-mended a coordination of the work of JSBC with the Association's Baptist Center, located at 400 East Chestnut Street.[11] Throughout the 1970s, the Baptist Center had become the Association's high-est budget category by a nearly three-to-one ratio of any of its other ministries.[12] The Baptist Center hosted a growing Day Care pro-gram, but due to financial shortfalls of the Association, the Center faced a sudden struggle of budget reductions.[13] In 1981, the Asso-ciation's Executive Committee appointed Jim Holladay as pastor/ director of the two Baptist centers' combined work, although each ministry continued to maintain its own facilities.[14] Holladay was a pastor at East Baptist Church who had previously coordinated programs at the Baptist Center during the 1970s.

Commemorating the centennial anniversary of the Jefferson Street Baptist Chapel in his report to the Long Run Association, Holladay stated:

> "No matter what the name, the inner city mission work of Long Run Baptists has had but one aim, to preach the good news to the poor to proclaim freedom for the prisoners and recovery of sight to the blind, to release the oppressed, and to proclaim the acceptable year of the Lord."[15]

The consolidated work was briefly known as the Baptist Centers Ministry program, with three major divisions of its work entailing a weekday program, a child care ministry, and the congregational programs conducted at the East Baptist Church and the Jefferson Street Baptist Chapel. Vacation Bible School ministries met at both campus locations, although funding the Day Care program, which carried over from the previous Baptist Center, continued to be a massive financial challenge. In 1981, the Jefferson Street congregation came under the sponsorship of Holladay's East Baptist Church, which donated $1,500 to the Chapel in its first year of the arrangement.[16] Under Holladay's direction, Michael Elliott became the designated pastor for the Jefferson Street Chapel's congregation in 1981 after having served in an interim pastorate capacity with the chapel the previous year.[17]

In July 1983, the consolidated Baptist Centers Ministry once more became distinct entities after the Long Run executive board approved a recommendation of the Baptist Centers Committee to appoint separate pastor/director positions for each of the two centers. Holladay continued at East while Elliott received greater control over the ministries of Jefferson Street Baptist Chapel.[18] Elliott's tenure as JSBC pastor/director lasted until 1987 and involved an increasingly tense working relationship with the Long Run Baptist Association.

As Chapel pastor/director, Elliott focused upon building tight bonds of fellowship with the congregation and emphasized social services to the neighborhood. According to Elliott, JSBC offered seventy programs of service in order to meet the diverse spiritual, social, emotional, and recreational needs of the community.[19] The Chapel hosted thousands of meals for homeless men and women while providing gospel presentations for visitors, and it cooperated with the local Community Treatment Center to host individuals serving time for drug and alcohol related charges at worship services. In 1983, JSBC provided job training and offered General Educational Development classes through the National Unemployed People's Association whereby the unemployed could upgrade their vocational skills to make themselves competitive candidates in the job market. [20] The following year, the Chapel began a "New-Start" program focused on helping newly converted Christians struggling with drug abuse and addictions.[21]

Elliott advocated homelessness awareness within the city, pushing for public policy changes by serving on a task force appointed by Louisville's mayor to study the nature of the problem. He allowed Jeff Street Chapel to serve as a temporary headquarters for Project Independence, which advocated fair energy legislation to guarantee a service plan for people who were not able to pay their utility bills.[22] The JSBC budget allowance from the Long Run Baptist Association grew substantially throughout the 1980s, from $57,259 in 1980 to $84,211 in 1989.[23]

Elliott became a popular pastor with the Chapel congregation, but his progressive views on subjects like economics and women in ministry clashed with conservatives in the Southern Baptist Convention.[24] In 1984, he hired Cindy J. Weber onto the JSBC staff as an associate pastor and coordinator of social services; after her election she lived in an apartment on the JSBC campus. When Elliott resigned his Chapel position in the spring of 1987, Weber was ideally positioned to succeed him as pastor/director at Jefferson Street. The Long Run Baptist Association, however, would not approve the promotion of Weber, and she remained employed in an interim role for the next four years as the Association struggled to decide how to fill the position.

The Parting

Throughout the 1980s, the Southern Baptist Convention experienced a cultural and political battle between the conservative/ fundamentalist and moderate/liberal wings of its theological spectrum. In 1979, theologically conservative Southern Baptists won their first political victory in the ideological war for the denomination's theological future by electing Adrian Rogers as convention president at its annual meeting. Rogers's candidacy included a passionate affirmation of biblical inerrancy—that the Scriptural canon is fully inspired by God and completely free from error—as a central tenant in Southern Baptist life.[25] The office of SBC president carried the power to appoint like-minded Baptists to the convention's Committee on Committees, which subsequently appointed persons into leadership positions throughout the denomination's various institutions. After a decade of electing conservative pastors to the SBC presidency, the effects of successive appointments had shifted the ideology of the denomination's leadership structure accordingly.

Undergirding the conservatives' agenda was an absolute commitment to biblical inerrancy, as any deviance upon this point should disqualify one from service within the denomination. Furthermore, the belief in biblical inerrancy led to the logical application of the principle that the Bible ought to be interpreted as literal truth to be obeyed by Christians and churches living under the covenant of the New Testament. Consequently, most Southern Baptist inerrantists also believed the correct interpretation and application of biblical revelation required a commitment to "complementarianism"—a contemporary name for a traditional view of appropriate gender relationships within the family and the church. Complementarian interpretations of passages like Ephesians 5:22, Colossians 3:18, 1 Timothy 2:12, and 1 Peter 3:1 affirmed that God's intention for the office of church pastors should be limited to men possessing the qualifications stated in the texts.[26] In 1984, the Southern Baptist Convention narrowly passed a resolution affirming its position that women should not pastor churches or serve in other leadership roles entailing ordination.[27]

In 1993, The Southern Baptist Theological Seminary elected R. Albert Mohler, Jr., an outspoken affirmer of both biblical inerrancy and complementarianism, as its president. Mohler succeeded Roy L. Honeycutt, who had pushed unsuccessfully to advance the cause of egalitarianism—the belief that gender should not be a qualification for ministerial service—in denominational and church leadership structures throughout the past decade.[28] Mohler's early years as president of the seminary were characterized by intense conflicts between his conservative aims for the institution and the more liberal, egalitarian culture which had entrenched itself at the institution for decades.[29]

Michael Elliott and Cindy Weber both earned degrees from Southern Seminary under the Honeycutt administration. Both believed that egalitarianism should have a future in Southern Baptist institutions, but the denomination's shifting political climate made that vision look like an increasingly unlikely outcome. Under the "interim" title, Weber served as the Jefferson Street Baptist

Chapel's functional director and pastor from 1987 – 1989, but the Long Run Baptist Association refused to promote her to the head position.

F. Russell Bennett was the Long Run Association's executive director, and he opposed the promotion of Weber to the head director/pastorate of the Chapel. Weber, beloved by the Jefferson Street congregation, desired for the Chapel to achieve greater independence from the Long Run Association so that it might function as an autonomous local Baptist church. Bennett and Weber's working relationship became tumultuous during the late 1980s, as Bennett believed that Weber and the Chapel were disrespecting the rights and authority of the Association. Weber and her congregation believed the Association's involvement was constraining their mission work to the community.[30]

Bennett's conflict with Weber owed more to personal and political considerations than it did ideological difference. Bennett was a longtime denominational servant of the Long Run Baptist Association, who held the Executive Director position between 1981 and 1998. He possessed no affinity for the doctrine of biblical inerrancy, considering it a blasphemous "deification of Scripture."[31] Furthermore, he had no sympathy for the series of political victories the conservatives were experiencing during the denomination's national meetings throughout the 1980s.[32]

Bennett was preeminently concerned with navigating the Association's ministries safely around the denomination's political landmines, and wanted to avoid the question of women in ministry becoming an explosive liability for the Long Run Association. Though Bennett may have respected Weber's competence and dedication to the Chapel, he recommended her talents be used as a weekday director of events rather than as the JSBC's public face in the head pastorate. In a statement printed in the *Western Recorder*, Bennett explained his disagreement with Weber and the Chapel:

"The association has not acted against any church that has ordained women as deacons or as ministers. That has been settled. But there are churches in our association that do not believe women ought to serve as ordained pastors. It's not fair to ask them to support (through associational ministries) something they think is biblically wrong. I do not share their sentiments, but I do not want to offend my 'weaker brother.' "[33]

The conflict between the Chapel and the Long Run Association reached an impasse. Under pressure from Bennett, Weber resigned her interim pastorate in March 1989, and the Long Run committee responsible for oversight of JSBC soon divided the Chapel's leadership duties between Weber, who continued as inter-director, and a committee-appointed interim pastor.[34] Weber, however, continued to function as the congregation's associate pastor and shared duties with the Long Run Association's interim-pastors; although the Association's annual reports did not identify her as such.

This compromise became a source of further contention within the Association, as both Bennett and the Long Run Personnel Committee did not favor a division of the JSBC leadership positions as a wise long-term plan. Furthermore, the Home Mission Board of the Southern Baptist Convention cut its funding for the interim pastor position at the Chapel on account of the gender issue. The Kentucky Baptist Convention also withdrew funding after learning that Weber was both preaching and baptizing at JSBC chapel services.[35]

The JSBC congregation, loyal to Weber, desired autonomy from the Long Run Association so that it could have full authority to make personnel decisions. The congregation unanimously desired a complete separation, financial and otherwise, of all church and center staff positions. It voted to install Weber as its senior pastor in September of 1991 with the approval of the JSBC Committee, but the Association evicted the congregation from the 733 East Jefferson Street building.[36] After some negotiations between the JSBC Committee and the Long Run Executive Board, the Association granted Weber and her congregation up to one year to comply with the request as they searched for adequate facilities with some support from the JSBC Committee, chaired by Jim England.[37] The congregation vacated the property and found a replacement location one block south on East Liberty Street, christening itself as the Jeff Street Baptist Community at Liberty.

Social Services, Federal Funding, and 21st Century Challenges

With the parting of the Jeff Street congregation from the Long Run Baptist Association, the Association exclusively referred to the mission work conducted at the JSBC building as the Jefferson Street Baptist Center, dropping the moniker of "chapel" as the Center's work no longer resembled the typical ministries of a local church. The Association hired Steve Golden—a Southern Baptist home missionary who had a decade of experience in Christian social ministry—as the new JSBC director.[38] Golden served from 1991 until 1994, striving to refocus the Center's work upon meeting the needs of families and the homeless within the community.[39] He received assistance from Paul Whiteley, who coordinated homeless ministries and remained with the Center after the departure of Weber's congregation.

During the 1990s, JSBC continued its social services ministry in providing shelter, food, utilities, clothing, and medical needs for individuals and families. Extensive repairs were also made to the JSBC building's bathroom facilities and roof replacement, as necessary additional funding was solicited through a direct appeal to the churches of the Association.[40] The Phoenix Project, coordinated by Whiteley, allowed for temporary housing of homeless men within the center's facility while also providing laundry and hygiene services, haircuts, and mail services.[41] Participants of the Phoenix Project, up to eight men at one time, were allowed to reside within the Center for up to eighteen months. The Center's staff offered the residents drug and alcohol rehabilitation, provided education and job-finding assistance, and taught each resident life skills related to shopping, meal preparation, cooking, and money management.[42]

Though the Center no longer offered a congregational ministry, it provided regular Bible studies, prayer meetings, and a Christian community which led some residents and visitors to make professions of Christian faith. During weekdays, homeless individuals could take advantage of drop-in services to receive access to coffee, a clothes closet, a storage room for up to two bags of personal belongings, laundry services, and a shower facility.[43] The Center encouraged Kentucky churches to assist its efforts through either buying, preparing, or serving meals on weekends, as it served Saturday lunch and Sunday breakfast to nearly 1,000 people a month while many other city soup kitchens closed over the weekend.[44]

Randall Harvey succeeded Golden as JSBC executive director upon the latter's resignation in August 1994. Harvey's term lasted until 2002, and it entailed substantial changes to the organization's structure and funding channels. Over the course of his administration, JSBC served over one hundred clients a day and converted many of its rooms into overnight living quarters for dozens of transitional clients at a time. Cooperation with government aid groups enhanced the service programs offered at JSBC, as well as its budgetary scope. In addition to social services and charitable aid, Bible studies and Sunday worship services presented the Christian gospel to visitors and residents.[45]

In a concerted effort to aid the chronic mentally ill, JSBC and Seven Counties Services established a new transitional living program in 1996. Dubbing it "The Fresh Start," the program provided beds for twelve homeless men suffering from mental illness in order to provide a safe, supportive opportunity for the men to learn stability and skills to pursue more permanent community housing. The program required residents to follow prescribed treatment plans provided by local agencies with the goal of helping the men move into personal apartments or supported housing programs.[46]

After renovating and expanding its bathroom and laundry services, the Center opened a day shelter in 1998.[47] The day shelter provided breakfast, coffee, clothing, and other necessities for homeless men and women during mornings.[48] The Center raised sufficient funds to convert its old sanctuary into additional rooms for residential housing, and the excess space allowed participation in "White Flag," whereby twenty additional clients were granted overnight emergency housing whenever the wind chill dipped below 35 degrees Fahrenheit.[49]

In 1997, the Jefferson Street Baptist Center became an incorporated entity with approval from the Long Run executive committee.[50] The JSBC committee transitioned into a board of directors, although the Association's Nominating Committee still maintained responsibility for electing members to the board from churches associated with the Long Run Association. The Association tasked the JSBC Board of Directors with the responsibilities of overseeing the physical and financial maintenance of the Center, advising the Long Run executive director regarding staff hires, delegating mission responsibilities to the JSBC director, and interceding toward God in prayer on behalf of its needs.[51]

As it entered the 21st century, JSBC defined its mission solely upon providing residential and support services to dually-diagnosed homeless individuals suffering from severe mental illness and substance abuse, dropping its programs for children and youth.[52] It significantly revamped and expanded its property to include facilities for U. S. Department of Housing and Urban Developing (HUD), constructing an addition to the rear of the existing facility with eleven apartments, two community rooms, laundry services, and office space.[53] These additions were funded largely by an increased amount of federal aid, the cost of which tallied around $700,000 when construction completed in late 2003.[54] Residents of the HUD housing apartments, many of whom received government disability checks, paid a monthly rent to the JSBC.

Although JSBC continued to receive annual budgetary allowances of nearly $90,000 from the Long Run Baptist Association, the expanding social ministry programs required it to secure additional funding. Gifts came from local churches and denominational offices outside of Kentucky. Grants came from non-profit charities and government sources.[55]

After Harvey's departure to pastor a church in North Carolina, the JSBC Board of Directors promoted as his successor Rick Brenny, who had been on the JSBC staff as a director of social service ministries since the mid-1990s.[56] Brenny, a recognized missionary of the North American Mission Board, continued overseeing the various homeless ministries implemented over the previous decade, and placed great emphasis upon personal evangelism of the Center's clients.

Brenny encouraged and aided Center residents and visitors toward spiritual and economic improvement:

> "We want our guests to become more employable and to gain permanent housing. We don't want to make it easy to be homeless, but we want to make it easier for them to get off the streets. Our desire is to build real and trusting relationships with those whom we serve so when the

opportunity to present the gospel arises, our guests will be honest with us and with God in their responses."[57]

PERSEVERANCE OF THE MISSION

Brenny built a favorable rapport with some of Louisville's most vibrantly evangelical Baptist congregations in the downtown district. He was able to instill trust in the Jefferson Street Baptist Center's theological direction with conservative, missions-focused churches that had developed a distant relationship with the Long Run Baptist Association after decades of moderate Baptist leadership. Local Baptist churches like Sojourn Community Church in Louisville reached out to aid the Center through coordinated volunteer work. Sojourn's pastor Daniel Montgomery explained his congregation's interest in working with the inner-city mission: "Our goal is to provide a mercy ministry here, not a disconnect like a mission trip, but ministry connected with the local church."[58]

Jesse Eubanks, one of the volunteers from Sojourn, joined the JSBC staff in 2006. Eubanks launched and directed the HOPE program, offering immediate field training for aspiring missionaries (ages 18-29) to live at the Center for one year and gain a new perspective of inner-city homelessness. The Center hosted four volunteer missionaries at a time, each of whom devoted up to twenty-five weekly hours to living, serving, eating, and working alongside the homeless. HOPE missionaries served JSBC through day shelter work, custodial labor, writing grants, and speaking to churches.[59]

John Ferguson, Brenny's successor, continued the trend of providing vocal evangelical leadership to the Jefferson Street Baptist Center, but this outspokenness came with a steep cost. During Ferguson's tenure as executive director, JSBC faced a severe financial crisis precipitated by successive severances of government funding. The financial crisis began in 2009 when the JSBC Board of Directors declined to accept a $50,000 grant from the U. S. Department of Housing and Urban Development. The HUD grant would have entailed approximately 10% of the Center's annual budget, but acceptance of the federal grant would have placed restrictions upon the organization's freedoms to present the Christian gospel to residents of the Fresh Start program.[60] The Center's Fresh Start program, under direction of Keith Parker, aided male participants in breaking cycles of addictions through Scriptural counseling, but the explicit religious element came into conflict with government regulations against proselytizing.

The *Western Recorder* published these details in a November 2009 article, which was in turn read by Andrew Bates, Planning and Research Supervisor for the Louisville Metro Government's Department of Housing & Family Services. Bates emailed Ferguson to inform him that the JSBC Fresh Start program was ineligible for Emergency Shelter Grant funding, according to federal regulation that organizations directly funded under the ESG program "may not engage in inherently religious activities, such as worship, religious instruction, or proselytization as part of the programs or services funded under this part."[61]

Although JSBC could have continued to exercise their religious commitments to persons in the day shelter, neither the directors nor the staff would willingly accept any restrictions upon sharing the gospel with all clients without discrimination. Bates—who identified as a Baptist himself—insisted that such practices constituted improper proselytizing and an abuse of the principle of the separation of church and state.[62] Consequently, the Louisville Metro Government withdrew funding for JSBC, which amounted to an annual loss of nearly $28,000.

Over the next three years, JSBC sank deeper into a perilous financial state. The Center also suffered the effects of declining contributions by local churches with the Long Run Baptist Association, a loss Ferguson estimated at $3,000 in 2009.[63] With declining denominational giving and the stripping of government aid, JSBC had to endure without sufficient funding from its two most reliable sources of income.

Because of the budgetary deficits, JSBC had to redirect funds for various ministries in order to keep the facility open and operational. The HOPE program suffered in particular, as money originally budgeted to support residential missionary training ended up being used to pay the building's utility bills.[64] The Fresh Start program was retooled and renamed LifeChange, offering a nine-to-twelve month residential care and counseling program for homeless men estranged from family due to "life-dominating sins." After Ferguson departed, the Center found itself without a full-time executive director, so Jesse Eubanks stepped into the interim role.

Despite the dark cloud that lingered over the Center's future, a silver lining appeared in July 2012 in the form of a bequest. Even this opportunity brought frustration, however, as the terms of the bequest were unclear if the full amount should go to JSBC or the Jeff Street Baptist Community at Liberty, Cindy Weber's congregation headquartered at 800 East Liberty Street. Ultimately, both parties settled on receiving a portion of the original amount. After its legal fees, JSBC's portion of the bequest was far less than it could have been, but it helped sustain the ministry's operations until larger donations could be secured.[65]

In spite of the Center's mounting troubles, its sacrificial evangelical public witness continued to endear itself to the theologically conservative, missions-focused Christians and Baptist congregations of Louisville. In 2012, Bryce Butler joined the JSBC Board of Directors, and engineered a successful strategy that brought the ministry back from the brink of bankruptcy. Butler brought shrewd and creative financial expertise to the organization's leadership team, having experience in strategic investing and advising non-profit organizations. Through networking, Butler secured a grant from a private donor in excess of $100,000. This grant stabilized JSBC financial footing for the remainder of the year.[66]

Local churches who sympathized with the work of the organization answered the Center's call for special offerings, with Southeast Christian Church donating a substantial amount comparable to the private grant secured by Butler.[67] The Noltemeyer real estate company announced a campaign to match all donations up to $50,000 given to the Center.[68] JSBC also raised funds by appealing for charitable gifts from the general public. These donations allowed JSBC to both survive and invest in renovations and security enhancements to the facility's kitchen, baggage storage area, and the front entrance.[69]

The JSBC Board of Directors pegged Phil Schultz to fill the vacancy of executive director near the end of 2012. Schultz brought nearly two decades of experience in Christian rescue mission work to the position, further instilling confidence in the ministry's supporters that JSBC was well positioned to bounce back from its multi-year financial crisis. Schultz led the Center to join the Association of Gospel Rescue Missions, which consisted of theologically like-minded institutions with experience in homeless ministry and fund-raising. The alliance provided a network of support that allowed for greater training of the JSBC staff as well as a long-desired boost in morale.

MISSION FOR THE FUTURE

After this serendipitous turn of events, the Jefferson Street Baptist Center stood on firm financial footing by the end of 2012, having persevered through one of the most difficult crises in its 130-year history.[70] Its Board of Directors recognized that significant changes were still necessary to ensure its best positioning for future success. One obvious hurdle was the very name of the ministry, which placed emphasis upon a single city street and frequently led to branding confusion with the Jeff Street Baptist Community at Liberty. The JSBC Board of Directors believed the name confusion had resulted in loss of potential donations, with the 2012 bequest settlement being the most notable recent example.

The Board of Directors submitted a proposal to R. Wesley Pitts, Executive Director of Missions for the Long Run Baptist Association, to file a DBA to operate under a name more in line with its ministry focus for the city of Louisville and the region of Southern Indiana.[71] The new name, Louisville Rescue Mission, became the public designation after an unveiling ceremony in front of the facility on September 4, 2014.

At its April 2, 2015 fundraising banquet, the Mission initiated a new tradition of presenting the Holcombe Mercy Ministry Award, to be given annually to an individual who best exemplifies the vision of the Mission's founder in helping Louisville's hurting and homeless. Bryce Butler received the inaugural award for his services rendered to the Mission during his term on the Board of Directors.[72] In 2015, the Louisville Rescue Mission operated with an annual budget in excess of one million dollars, with the majority of its revenue provided through individual donations, foundations and grants, and local churches.

EPILOGUE

A Conclusion,
but Not the Final Word

At the completion of this writing, the Louisville Rescue Mission exists to extend gospel-centered mercy to the homeless and hurting of the greater Louisville area. Its core values stress the principles of community, transformation, and Jesus Christ as the source of all eternal hope, purpose, love, and life. Its incumbent executive director is Cory Bledsoe, who oversees a team of dedicated program managers and volunteers. Its Board of Directors, currently presided over by Vince Scarbrough, consists of Christian professionals who volunteer their services to offer governance, guidance, accountability, and support to the Mission.

The Mission continues to offer emergency day shelter services to the homeless, a nine-month addiction recovery program for men focused on life-transformation with a biblical foundation, and learning center services for residents offering over 375 hours of vocational training. The Board of Directors hopes to expand its ministries into southern Indiana and open a day shelter for women in the near future. The Mission is in constant need of donations of toiletry and cleaning supplies as well as volunteer workers and preachers. Churches can assist the Mission through sending small group volunteers, scheduling mission trips, and driving collections for seasonal items such as warm clothing, school supplies, food, hygiene products, and holiday gifts for residents.

Throughout its long and eventful history, the work of the Mission has never been without great challenges and adversity. On multiple occasions, it has faced crises in leadership and financial stability. The contemporary stewards of the Mission's administration affirm that the Mission's remarkable endurance owes all thanksgiving to the sovereign and merciful will of God. This historical overview demonstrates that the perseverance of the Mission also owes great appreciation to dedicated individuals whose commitment to the work of gospel mission ministry motivated them to make great personal sacrifices on behalf of the ministry. After nearly 135 years, the Mission maintains a fervent evangelical witness to downtown Louisville. Financial considerations have always been a crucial component in the institution's survival, but its endurance owes to the resolve of Christians who believed Louisville would be better with the Mission than without it. Though the Mission's work has always been accomplished by an ensemble, the talent and devotion of a few individuals sets an inspiring precedent for others to follow.

At the 135th anniversary of the Mission's establishment, the story of Steve P. Holcombe—the converted gambler—continues to inspire the current supporters of the Louisville Rescue Mission. If ever there lived a man who pursued his passions with almost unrestrained ferocity, it was Holcombe. For over forty years, he was consumed by personal pride and chased after the thrill of gambling. The last three decades of his life, however, were consumed by an even greater passion for preaching the biblical gospel to destitute men and making every feasible effort to help in their life reformations. Though far from a perfect man—even after his conversion, his zealousness for mission work may have made him a poor administrator and difficult to work with—Holcombe's enduring legacy is a powerful testimony of how faith in Jesus Christ transforms not only a man but also the man's culture.

The catalyst behind Holcombe's own spiritual transformation came about when a young minister named Gross Alexander referred to a weathered, middle-aged man as "brother" during a seemingly chance encounter. It is unlikely that Alexander had the gift of peering into Holcombe's soul when he spoke that simple word in 1877, but the Methodist minister possessed an evangelical hope which allowed him to view men beyond their present state, envisioning who they might become through the transformative power of Jesus Christ supplemented by Christian friendship. Together with his wife, Alexander invested himself into Holcombe's life, making almost every effort to ensure that the seeds of faith sown yielded good fruit. Holcombe, in turn, invested the rest of his life imitating his pastor's example throughout the city of Louisville.

Throughout the various decades and eras of the Mission's history, it has ministered to countless individuals of diverse backgrounds. It has served men and women, children and the elderly, people of every race and various nationalities. It has proclaimed the gospel to its visitors and residents through the use of charitable and government funds, but it has learned to survive without such aid. For over seventy years, it has been nourished by the generosity of Southern Baptist churches in particular, and the Mission's theological commitment remains cognizant with the doctrinal confession of the Baptist Faith and Message 2000.

Holcombe envisioned a downtown rescue mission that would provide regular evangelical proclamation and aid to the city's most desperate and destitute citizens, who would not otherwise be sufficiently served by most traditional congregations. In Holcombe's day, businessmen and civic leaders recognized the social benefits of such an endeavor, knowing from experience that genuine spiritual transformation typically results in better citizens who make useful contributions to society.

Today, the Louisville Rescue Mission continues to focus its resources on aiding the homeless to rise up from their addictions, illnesses, and dependencies. The homeless and transitional-living population of "Kentuckiana," the Louisville metropolitan area, totals around 9,000 people, and up to 1,600 may find themselves unsheltered on any given night.[1] The Mission desires to combat the problem of homelessness by teaching its residents and visitors a holistic response that begins and ends with a biblical definition of humanity and a proper relationship between God and humanity.

"The Gambler's Mission" has proven to be an investment which has yielded compound interest. It is still needed in Louisville, perhaps even more today than at any other point in its history. Thus, this history of the Louisville Rescue Mission's first 135 years concludes, with the hope that its best days are yet to come, so long as God wills.

APPENDIX A

Selected Messages from
Steve P. Holcombe

"God's Love for Sinners"
Romans 5:8: "But God commendeth His love for us in that while we were yet sinners, Christ died for us."

There are many of us who *feel* that we are *sinners*, who know it, and who do not want any proof of it; but we can't be persuaded to believe that God has any love for us or interest in us. We have gotten to be such wicked sinners that maybe our friends have forsaken us, and we can not believe that God has any feeling of tenderness for us. We are willing to admit that God loves good people, those who are obedient, and that if we were good, He would *then* love us; but as it is, He can not love us, and there is no reason why He should love us. And then we go back and try to call up all our sins; all the times when we rejected Christ and the truth, and we find plenty of arguments to prove that God does not love us.

But stop! You are judging the great God by yourself. You know you would not love one who would have treated you as you have treated God, and so you conclude He does not love you. You find it *exceedingly* hard to believe in the love of God. This is one of the sad effects of sin. It darkens our hearts and separates us far, far from

God, so that when we come to feel our need of Him we have no confidence that He will accept us or help us.

Besides, by your long service of sin, you have put yourself in the power of an enemy who makes it as difficult as possible for you to *believe* in God's love for you. But I come to you today with a declaration and assurance from God's own word, that though you have been a sinner all your life, and still feel that you are the greatest of sinners, the great God loves you with a true, deep, warm and yearning love.

The great proof of it is the life and death of Jesus Christ, His Son. Have you read about it in the Gospel? Ah, if you had, and had seen Him delighting to be with the poor and the outcast, eating with them, choosing them for His friends, speaking words of heavenly cheer to them, pronouncing their sins forgiven and promising them heaven, then you would be moved and attracted and convinced. And then if you had read the pathetic story of His awful sufferings and death, and had reflected that "He was wounded for our transgressions; He was bruised for our iniquities; all we like sheep have gone astray, and the Lord hath laid on Him the iniquity of us *all*," then hope would begin to dawn in your breast, and faith in His love would not be so difficult. But you have neglected to read and reflect about it, and so I am come to bring the glad tidings to you where you are, and to beg you to believe it for your own sake.

And now, here are some of the ways God has taken to tell you of His love: Psalm 103:13; Isaiah 49:15; Luke 11:13; Luke 18:13-14; Luke 15:7, 10; Prodigal Son; Luke 7:36 to end.

"I came not to call the righteous but *sinners* to repentance."

Why does God, in so many ways, express His love for sinners?

"Godliness Profitable for This Life"
1 Timothy 4:8: "But godliness is profitable unto all things having the promise of the life that now is and of that which is to come."

There are not many who think this. Nearly everybody admits that religion is a good thing to have when he is about to die and to enter upon the future life; and all men, however hardened in vice, wickedness and crime, have a sure expectation and firm intention of making some preparation for death and what may follow death. They fully intend to make amends to conscience for the violations of it, of which they have been guilty.

There are men here today who know that this is true of themselves, who feel that the coffin and the grave and the unknown future beyond are the most fearful of realities, and who are firmly persuaded that a day of reckoning is coming, maybe slowly, but surely, and they do mean to make peace in some way with conscience before that time draws near. And so I say all men agree that religion is good for death and what is to follow; but how it can be an advantage to one in *this life,* they can not see.

But godliness is a help to a man in making a living. If a man is honest, industrious, faithful and conscientious, he will be in demand. Such men are always in demand; and, when they are known, can get employment and can keep employment; but a man who is a true Christian *is* honest, industrious, careful, temperate, trustworthy and conscientious, because he works and lives not to please men but God. Hence, such a one is always wanted. Employers, rather than give up such men, will increase their salaries and offer them extra inducements. A Main Street merchant found he could not do without Willie Holcombe conveniently, so he raised his salary twenty dollars a month rather than lose him.

And, even if they are among strangers, and not known, yet God will turn the hearts of strangers toward them, as he turned the heart of the prison-keeper in Egypt toward Joseph. And when they have a chance to *try* and to show their value, their employers will not give them up.

But then if a man is in business for himself, he will get a large custom if people find out that he does business as a Christian—that is, he does not charge an unjust and exorbitant price, his goods are only what he says they are, he gives full and honest measure, his word can be trusted, he will correct mistakes and take back an article if it is found not to be good. Show people such a man and they will all want to patronize him. William Kendrick was such a man here in Louisville.

The Christian man has the *promise of God* that he shall be provided for (Matthew 6: 32, 33), while the godless man has no such assurances at all.

But religion keeps a man from those vices which destroy the health—as dissipation, debauchery, intemperance, etc.—and health is one of the chief elements in human happiness. Religion keeps men also from those crimes which bring men into ruin and disgrace and bitter remorse. Many a man has come to the jail or penitentiary or gallows who would have escaped it all if he had had religion to protect and shield and restrain and assist him. And many a good and happy man there is who might have been a guilty criminal and a wretched convict but for the grace of God and the lessons and blessings of true religion. He might gradually have been led off and on and on till he would have become capable of committing any crime. I might have been a drunkard or a murderer still, if God had not changed my heart and helped me mightily and constantly by His grace.

But religion takes away the fear of death and the dread of the future and gives inward and constant peace—a heart happiness which poverty and disappointment and trials can not destroy. And nothing else can do this but true religion. Religion can release a man from the power of those evil habits which make a man's life miserable— from acquired appetites, as drinking, opium eating, debauchery, licentiousness, swearing, gambling and even from tobacco.

Religion makes a good father, a good mother, a good husband, a good wife, good children, it makes the family happy, and the home bright, cheerful, joyous. It makes a man a good citizen. So he can get along in peace with his neighbors and even become a peace-maker among them when they quarrel.

Thus have I tried to show you that, regardless of the future, godliness is profitable for this life. But if this were not so, if the life of a Christian were an uninterrupted experience of pains and disappointments and sorrows, yet, in view of the interests of the soul, and the possibilities of the future, and the length of eternity, it would be the highest wisdom to cheerfully accept all these and endure them to the bitter end, in order to depart out of this world with a peaceful and un accusing conscience and a sure preparation for heaven.

O man, what will you do with eternity, *eternity*, if you go thither unprepared? Did you ever try to think of eternity? As John Wesley says, "If a bird were to come once in a million of years and take away one grain of the earth, when it had taken the whole earth away, that would not be eternity, nor the beginning of eternity." And it is certain that eternity is the period of the desolation and confusion and remorse and suffering of the lost.

But even if we had to live in misery all this life, it would be better to do it and have religion; for it alone fits us for happiness in the life to come. Take away property, comforts, friends, family, reputation, health, but give me religion, and I shall have a passport into the kingdom of heaven and an eternity of rest and blessedness.

O then, come to Jesus Christ and have all these things and heaven beside.

Matthew 11:28: "Come unto me all ye that labor and are heavy laden and I will give you rest."

The cry of all hearts is for rest, for contentment.

Not only does the heart of humanity cry out for rest, rest, rest; their busy and tired hands and feet *toil* for it day and night, year in and year out.

It is for this that men labor through the days and weeks of summer's heat and expose themselves to the severities of winter's cold.

It is for this that they plow and sow and reap and gather into barns.

It is for this that they blow the bellows and swing the heavy hammers from morn until night.

It is for this they buy and sell and buy again to sell again.

It is for this that men will spend years of toil in schools and colleges, burning the midnight lamp till the eye is heavy and the brain is tired.

It is for this that they will leave wife and children to try their fortunes in some distant California or Australia.

It is for this they will abandon their homes in time of war to brave the dangers of the battlefield.

It is for this that they will worry away the hours of night in games to get each other's money.

It is for this they will devise schemes and lay plans to entrap their fellows, sometimes going to the length of committing murder.

It is for this that women will toil with the needle and bend over the sewing machine.

It is for this they will stand for weary hours behind counters measuring off goods or waiting for customers to buy.

It is for this that they work over the hot stove or wear out their hands in the wash-tub.

Yes, it is for this that some of them, weary of work-life, will venture on the slippery paths of pleasure, turn their thoughts toward the gilded chambers of licentiousness, sell virtue and abandon home and family to go in the ways that in the end take hold on death and hell.

We are a race of *toilers.* All over the world it is the same. We see it here in Louisville. It is work, work, work, go, go, go.

And are we happy? Have we rest?

But not only are we toiling, some in one way, some in another; some by innocent means, some by wicked means; some by what does no harm to ourselves or our neighbor, and some by what does harm to both, in order to obtain rest and happiness; it is also true that most of us are heavy laden, oppressed and saddened beneath burdens that we cannot shake off, cannot get rid of.

Some of us are bowed down under our poverty. No good house to live in, no comfortable home to turn into after the battles and toils of outside life, no comfortable shelter for our families. No assurance as to where we are to get tomorrow's bread. No comfortable and respectable clothes to wear, and, of course, no friends. For when a poor fellow gets poor and shabby, his friends drop off and pass by on the other side. No friends, none of that sympathy and communion of friendship which all human hearts so crave and which they find to be the best part of what this life can give.

Yes; some of us have this burden to bear. And then some of us are bowed down beneath some great sorrow, which may be one thing in one case and another in another. In some cases it is domestic trouble, continual jars and broils in the family, no peace, no quiet, no love. Ah, if we could see into all the homes in this city, I fear we should find in many of them family trouble of some sort. Or it may be some dear one of yours is given to drink or to gambling and is wearing out his life as fast as vice can eat it away, with no hope beyond the grave.

Ah, yes; no doubt some of *you* are yourselves the slaves of evil habits which you hate and would do anything to break off. You have tried by resolving and promising and all to no purpose; you have felt ashamed and degraded because you had no power to do what you felt you ought to do and what you knew would be infinitely better for you.

Do you not know men who would willingly give a right arm for deliverance from some degrading and ruinous habit? But giving a right arm avails nothing, nor any human effort or means.

Then, again some of you are bowed down by the recollection of your past life and its dissipation and crimes.

You may have mistreated father, mother, sister, and may have broken hearts by your cruelty that would gladly have bled for you. You may have crushed a loving and faithful wife by your selfishness and your brutality and heartlessness. You may have driven your children to desperation and crime by your coldness and hardness to them.

And maybe some life, innocent until you came upon it with your hellish art, has been corrupted and embittered and darkened by your base passions and lusts.

Maybe your hands have gone to that last extreme of human crime and have deprived a fellowman of life. And, oh, if any of these things be true, what must be the burden of remorse, remorse, remorse, that weighs upon your heart.

But you are the very ones whom Jesus addresses and invites in this tender appeal. Do you believe it? In the second place, consider who it is that offers you rest. It is one who knows you and who knows what you need and one who has all power in heaven and in earth to give what you need. Lastly, consider what this rest means which Jesus offers to you burdened and toiling ones. It is rest from sin, both its guilt and power. It is rest from all care. For He has said, we should cast all our care upon Him because He cares for us.

"PREPARATION FOR WINNING SOULS"
[Holcombe delivered this address before the Convention of Christian Workers of United States and Canada which met on September 21-28, 1887 at the Broadway Tabernacle, New York.]

I am sure, my dear brethren, that in the discussion of this topic we are to be allowed some liberty and some latitude; and, if I shall speak in a general way, I trust I shall not be counted out of order. And, not to detain you with preliminaries, I say that, to be a winner of souls, a man must have the anointing of the Holy One, reproducing the mind that was in Christ, who "though he was rich, yet *for* our sakes became poor, that we through His poverty might become rich," and who "being in the form of God, thought it not a usurpation to be equal with God, but He emptied Himself and took upon Him the form of a servant; and being found in fashion as a man, He humbled Himself and became obedient as far as unto death, even death on a cross."

A sympathy that arises from any other motive, or comes from any other source, than His divine and supernatural anointing, will fall short of the mark, and will be found too shallow and weak to bear with the hardheartedness, the perversity and the ingratitude of sinful men.

This anointing, on the other hand, brings with it a yearning love and a profound sympathy for those who are in the blindness and bondage of sin, which impels one to *seek out* the lost, to be at patient pains to save them, and to bear with all their dullness, slothfulness, selfishness, perverseness and thanklessness, while they are under training, so to speak.

It makes a man as ready and anxious to save the soul of a solitary sinner, however humble and degraded he may be, as to preach with power to the great congregations. It was this that made John Wesley as willing and careful and patient in talking to a negro servant girl as to a multitude. And it was this which lead a greater than John Wesley to lead with patient love along, the poor Samaritan adulteress whom He met at the well of Jacob.

But what is more important and imperative for the immediate work of getting a dead soul to a living Saviour, this divine anointing imparts that peculiar and energetic pungency which pierces to the heart and conscience of a sinner, rouses his fears, and prepares him for the reception of Christ.

Not only so, this unction from the Holy One is accompanied with a practical wisdom and *insight* which discerns, if not all things, yet, at least, *many practical things*. It enables a man to see that the first thing to be done in the way of saving a sinner is to convict him of sin. To get him to admit theoretically that he is a sinner, is equal to zero, amounts to nothing. But, in a way not to repel him, he must be made to *feel* that he is sinful, and so, wretched. It is wonderful what tact some men have in this respect. Here lies, undoubtedly, the secret of Sam Jones' power. He turns all classes of men, Pharisees in the church and sinners out of it, inside out, and makes them see, in spite of all spiritual apathy and all self-deception, what they are. He shows them secrets which they thought nobody knew but themselves.

But a greater than he did the same thing—Jesus touched the *sore spot* in the conscience of the Samaritan woman and compelled her to say: "He told me all things that I have done." This revealing the secrets of the heart is a thing that fascinates and attracts and wins a sinner; and he feels, if you know so well without being told, all the particulars of his inner life and all the desperate trouble of his case, you surely cannot make a mistake in pointing out the way of escape. Just as a patient yields immediate and unquestioning confidence to the physician who can tell him all his symptoms and describe his feelings better than he himself can do it.

If preaching the love of Christ without convicting of sin would have saved people, then most people in the United States would have been saved long ago, for the love of Christ has been told and retold and preached and re-preached, and it does not bring sinners to repentance. To be sure there are some sinners who have found, by bitter experience, the ripe fruits of sin, and these may be already prepared to accept a deliverer and a deliverance as soon as offered to them.

The possession of this unction presupposes that a man is correct, upright, holy in his life; for God would not give it to one who was not so. I believe Mr. Moody was right when he said: "If a man's life is not above reproach, the less he says the better." A friend of mine says he knows a minister who, though no doubt a good man and a fine talker, will *lie* now and then. Of course, he would not call it lying, nor would his admirers call it lying, but lying it is; and so he has no power. His preaching is like a sounding brass and a tinkling cymbal.

There are some men who have some little success in soul-saving, but who would have much more success, if their lives were thoroughly holy, and Christ-like. And indeed some men would not have the success they do have, if the public knew their secret life. For example, there are some men who indulge evil thoughts (if they do not go further) and who are not chaste in their associations with women; and there are others who are ill-tempered, cross, fault-finding, sour and bitter in their home life. If these things were publicly and generally known, they would lose what power they have with the people. Brethren, we can hardly be too careful of these things. But a full and constant anointing of the Holy One would correct all these evils at the *source,* namely, in the heart. It makes a sober Christian man tremble to know how little some of the preachers and evangelists of the day *pray.* It would be no wonder if under stress of some sudden and strong temptation, they should fall into scandalous sin and disgrace themselves and the cause they represent. There is an old and true saying that "when a man's life is lightning, his words will be thunderbolts."

We are advised to make ourselves familiar with the Scriptures, to equip ourselves with weapons from the armory of God's word; and excellent advice it is. No man can maintain a spiritual life who does not habitually and diligently study God's holy word. No man is prepared to understand the wants of souls or to deal with them who is not familiar with the Scriptures. It is a marked characteristic of our honored brother, D. L. Moody, that he can, not only discern the deeper, inner spiritual sense of all the Scriptures, both of the Old Testament and the New, but he can handle and apply them with a skill, effectiveness and power that are truly wonderful. And, what is more, he is peculiarly apt in selecting just the right passages for any particular case or occasion. He is truly a masterly handler of the sword of the spirit, and his success is largely due to this fact.

But there is a class of workers who seem to think that it is sufficient to know by heart some Scriptures, or to have a certain facility in referring to different passages, and they rely upon this, congratulating themselves that they are doing well. But it is all perfunctory and lifeless and dead. There is no charm, no warmth, no power in it. A man must be more than a mechanical text-peddler in order to impress, arouse, comfort and save the souls of men. You may pitch cold lead at a man all day long and never break his skin; but let a full charge of ignited gunpowder drive it out of a well-aimed rifle, and the effect is terrific. So these text-mongers may throw Scripture at people all day long, and they laugh at it. But let the same missile be hurled forth with the energy of a soul on fire of the Holy Ghost, and the slain of the Lord will be many.

So, my brother, there is absolutely no substitute for this unction of the Holy Spirit. And this unction is given in answer to self-denying and daily prayer. If we would know the secret of power with men, we *must* spend much time in secret communion with God.

APPENDIX B

Testimonials from
the Staff of the
Louisville Rescue Mission

"During my years in the social services field I was constantly reminded that true transformation extends beyond behavior modification and must occur within the heart. The gospel teaches us that heart transformation is found in Christ and Christ alone. Louisville Rescue Mission is a place where true holistic ministry takes place as those experiencing homelessness are not only met with tangible supports but are introduced to the transforming power of the gospel of Jesus Christ. It is a humbling joy to be a part of what the Lord is doing at LRM."

Cory Bledsoe, Executive Director

—

"I work at LRM because I believe that everybody has purpose and value. The men and women that are shunned by society are dying on our streets both physically and spiritually. I work here in hopes that we may help them through the power of the Gospel."

Adam Fleming, Director of Operations

—

"Working at Louisville Rescue Mission has shown the blessing and heavy responsibility of representing our Lord to the hurting and downtrodden. Mixing rhythms of hope and grace for those who have caused extreme damage to themselves and others has been my relentless anthem and mission, and Louisville Rescue Mission is a special place where that mixing takes place. Seeing men recover from that damage and repairing the damage caused to others keeps driving me to my knees thanking the Lord for his kindness to all men."
Harrison Swadley, *LifeChange Program Manager*

—

"Being able to serve the people in need is a blessing from God. I feel our Staff and Volunteers are part of a team sharing God's love and putting a smile on the faces of the homeless and hurting men and women of Louisville. I have seen many changes here at Louisville Rescue Mission but one thing remains the same Jesus' name is boldly proclaimed."
Joanie Williams, *Day Shelter Coordinator*

—

"The Bible persistently commands the people of God to care for the poor. How do we obey this command? Louisville Rescue Mission is a beautiful place of blessing where poverty, addiction, and homelessness are tackled head on with the powerful gospel of Jesus Christ and in partnership with the local church. Sadly, such a ministry is a rare find. I am thankful for LRM and am blessed to watch God at work here."
Justin Compton, *Program Aide*

APPENDIX C

Original Constitution of the Union Gospel Mission (April 18, 1885)

Constitution

Name:
The name of the organization shall be The Union Gospel Mission of Louisville, KY.

Object:
The object shall be to do General Gospel City Missionary work to reach the masses, and to provide for the wants of those who need Christian teaching and encouragement.

Teaching:
The management and teaching shall be strictly evangelical and absolutely non-denominational.

Shall be Controlled by a Board of Managers:
The control of the Union Gospel Mission shall be exercised by a Board of Managers, composed of one lay-member from each Evangelical Congregation now existing or hereafter established in the City. The Board of Managers shall be self-perpetuating, and nine (9) shall constitute a quorum.

Executive Committee:
The Board of Managers shall select from their own number, annually an Executive Committee consisting of seven (7) members—but of these seven (7) there shall not be two (2) of the same denomination—who shall have (subject to the rules and regulations made by the Board of Managers) general control and oversight of the work in all its departments. The Executive Committee shall serve for one (1) year from the second Thursdays of April, and any vacancy occurring therein shall be filled by the Board of Managers. Five (5) members shall constitute a quorum of the Executive Committee.

Officers:
The officers of the organization shall be a President, Vice-President, Treasurer and Secretary, to be chosen by the Board of Managers at an annual meeting—to be held on the second Thursday of April in each year—to hold office for one year. The officers named may be chosen from the Board of Managers or otherwise, as Said Board may deem best. The President may be ex-officio a member of the Executive Committee.

Sub Committees:
The following Subcommittees shall be selected by the Executive Committee who shall serve for one year from the second Thursday in April. The Executive Committee shall select three Sub-Committees at their discretion; but the Chairman of each Sub-Committee shall be a member of the Executive Committee.

Finance Committee:
Shall consist of nine (9) members, five (5) constituting a quorum.

Devotional Committee: Shall consist of five (5) members, three (3) constituting a quorum.

Location and Rooms Committee: Shall consist of three (3) members, two (2) constituting a quorum.

Sunday School Committee: Shall consist of five (5) members, three (3) constituting a quorum.

Industrial School Committee: Shall consist of five (5) members, three (3) constituting a quorum.

Succession to Office:
All officers and committees, elected or appointed under this Constitution shall hold office until their successors are duly elected or appointed.

Amendments:
This Constitution may be altered and amended by a vote of 2/3 (two-thirds) of the Board of Managers present, written notice of such proposed alteration or amendment having been given each member thirty (30) days previously to such meeting.

NOTES

CHAPTER 1: THE PRODIGAL LIFE OF STEVE P. HOLCOMBE

1. Gross Alexander, *Steve P. Holcombe, The Converted Gambler: His Life and Work* (Louisville: Press of the Courier-Journal, 1888), 1.

2. Information obtained from Vanderbilt University course catalogs researched by Teresa Gray, Public Services Archivist, Special Collections & University Archives, Vanderbilt University, Nashville, Tennessee.

3. Horace M. Du Bose, *A History of Methodism 1881 – 1916* (Nashville: Publishing House of the M. E. Church South, 1916), 367-368.

4. Alexander consistently renders the name as "Shippingsport" in *Steve P. Holcombe, The Converted Gambler: His Life and Work.*

5. Ibid., 2.

6. Ibid., 2-3.

7. Ibid., 3-4.

8. "Romance of a Gambler turned Preacher," *Courier-Journal,* 10 October 1915; newspaper clipping glued into Minutes of the Union Gospel Mission, Volume 1, p. 97, [Manuscript documents relating to the Union Gospel Mission, Louisville, Ky.], Archives and Special Collections, James P. Boyce Centennial Library, The Southern Baptist Theological Seminary, Louisville, Kentucky.

9. Alexander, *Steve P. Holcombe, The Converted Gambler: His Life and Work*, 10.

10. Ibid., 5.

11. Ibid., 6.

12. Ibid., 6.

13. Ibid.

14. Ibid., 7.

15. Ibid.

16. Steve P. Holcombe, *The Story of Steve P. Holcombe: The Converted Gambler* (St. Louis: National Baptist Publication Co., 1896), 3.

17. Alexander, *Steve P. Holcombe, The Converted Gambler: His Life and Work*, 7-8.

18. Ibid., 11-12.

19. Ibid., 13.

20. Ibid., 14.

21. Ibid., 14-15.

22. Ibid., 16. Italics original to the cited reference.

23. Ibid., 15-18; "Romance of a Gambler turned Preacher," *Courier-Journal*, 10 October 1915.

24. Alexander, *Steve P. Holcombe, The Converted Gambler: His Life and Work*, 19.

25. A November 5, 1905 article published in the Sunday edition of an unidentified newspaper notes that "Steve P. Holcombe and Mrs. Holcombe will give an all-day reception Tuesday at the Holcombe Mission . . . in celebration of the golden anniversary of their wedding." Newspaper clipping is unattributed and glued onto a page of Union Gospel Mission minutes, Volume 1, 19.

26. Alexander, *Steve P. Holcombe, The Converted Gambler: His Life and Work*, 21.

27. Ibid., 21-22.

28. Ibid.

29. Ibid., 22-23.

30. Ibid., 41.

31. Ibid., 24-26.

32. Holcombe, *The Story of Steve P. Holcombe: The Converted Gambler*, 3.

33. Alexander, *Steve P. Holcombe, The Converted Gambler: His Life and Work*, 28-29.

34. Holcombe, *The Story of Steve P. Holcombe: The Converted Gambler*, 3-4.

35. Ibid., 4,

36. Ibid., 4-5.

37. Alexander, *Steve P. Holcombe, The Converted Gambler: His Life and Work*, 31.

38. Ibid., 33.

39. Ibid., 36.

40. Ibid., 39-40.

41. Holcombe, *The Story of Steve P. Holcombe: The Converted Gambler*, 4-5.

CHAPTER 2: THE CONVERTED GAMBLER AND THE HOLCOMBE MISSION

1. Gross Alexander, *Steve P. Holcombe, The Converted Gambler: His Life and Work* (Louisville: Press of the Courier-Journal, 1888), 42-43. Steve P. Holcombe, *The Story of Steve P. Holcombe: The Converted Gambler* (St. Louis: National Baptist Publication Co., 1896), 7.

2. Alexander, *Steve P. Holcombe, The Converted Gambler: His Life and Work*, 43.

3. Ibid., 44.

4. Ibid., 44-45.

5. Ibid., 45.

6. Ibid., 45.

7. Ibid., 46.

8. Holcombe, *The Story of Steve P. Holcombe: The Converted Gambler*, 9.

9. Alexander, *Steve P. Holcombe, The Converted Gambler: His Life and Work*, 47.

10. Ibid., 49-50.

11. Ibid., 53.

12. Ibid., 54.

13. This journal may now be lost to history, but its contents were recopied by Alexander in *Steve P. Holcombe, The Converted Gambler: His Life and Work*, 58-67.

14. Ibid., 61.

15. Ibid., 66.

16. Ibid., 68.

17. Ibid.

18. Ibid., 69.

19. Ibid., 383. Holcombe referenced this in a sermon titled "On Affliction and Suffering" from Lamentations 3:32-33.

20. Ibid., 399. This quote comes from an address Holcombe delivered at an April 1886 reunion of the converts of the Union Gospel Mission held at the Walnut-street Methodist Church.

21. Ibid., 72.

22. Ibid.

23. Ibid., 73-74.

24. Ibid.

25. Ibid., 72.

26. The Methodist church of Walnut Street is alternatively referred to as the "Fifth Street Methodist Episcopal Church South" and the "Fifth and Walnut Street Methodist church" in supplementary documents of the era.

27. Ibid., 80.

28. Ibid., 79.

29. Ibid., 80. Alexander includes the text of Morris's personal letter and first-hand memories of the mission's earliest years in pages 78-84 of *Steve P. Holcombe, The Converted Gambler: His Life and Work*.

30. Ibid., 81.

31. Ibid., 77.

32. Ibid., 77.

33. Ibid., 81.

34. Ibid., 81-82.

35. Ibid., 82-83.

36. Ibid., 83-84.

37. Ibid., xi.

38. Ibid., 83.

39. Ibid., 77. The Mission's first Board of Directors consisted of John L. Wheat, James G. Carter, P. H. Tapp, C. P. Atmore, and George W. Wicks.

40. Ibid., 85.

41. Ibid., 125.

42. Ibid.

43. Ibid., 83, 90.

44. Ibid., 90-91.

45. Ibid., 91.

46. Ibid., 93.

47. Ibid., 92.

48. Ibid., 92-93.

49. Ibid., 95.

50. Ibid., 96.

51. The Rev. Sam P. Jones became an additional supporter of the mission and worked with Holcombe to organize street preaching; Ibid., 84. Alexander also notes that even old gambling associations of Holcombe contributed over $500 to the mission's work; Ibid., 83. Many dramatic testimonies of men whose lives of vice were transformed through the ministry of Holcombe's mission are recounted in Alexander's biography, including the notable example of James "Whiskey Jim" Williams; Ibid., 86-89.

52. Ibid., 97.

53. Ibid., 96-97.

54. Ibid., 97-98.

55. Ibid., 98.

56. Ibid.

57. *Catalogue of The Southern Baptist Theological Seminary* (1881-82), 6.

58. *Catalogue of The Southern Baptist Theological Seminary* (1882-83), 8.

59. Alexander, *The Life and Work of Steve P. Holcombe: The Converted Gambler*, 74. Holcombe's letters to John A. Broadus from 1886, 1887, 1890, and 1894 are collected in the John A. Broadus Papers, Archives and Special Collections, James P. Boyce Centennial Library, Southern Baptist Theological Seminary, Louisville, Kentucky.

60. Alexander, "Letter from Dr. John A. Broadus," in *The Life and Work of Steve P. Holcombe: The Converted Gambler*, xiii.

Chapter 3: The Incorporation of the Union Gospel Mission

1. Union Gospel Mission, volume 1, preface, [Manuscript documents relating to the Union Gospel Mission, Louisville, Ky.], Archives and Special Collections of the James P. Boyce Centennial Library, The Southern Baptist Theological

Seminary, Louisville, Kentucky.

2. Ibid., 1.

3. *Notable Men of Kentucky at the Beginning of the Twentieth Century* (Louisville: George G. Fetter Printing Co., 1902), 188.

4. Union Gospel Mission, volume 1, 6-7.

5. Ibid., 9. Clancy was not one of the Mission's original constitutional committee, and is noted as a member from Walnut Street Baptist Church in the Mission's minute book. Ibid., 6.

6. Ibid., 7.

7. Ibid., 9-10. The original executive committee consisted of R. B. Porter, L. Richardson, J. T. Burghard, J. P. Torbitt, Clinton McClarty, P. Meguiar, and J. J. Broeg. The September 25, 1885 minutes of the Union Gospel Mission record that Harvey S. Irwin had been appointed to act as member of the committee in place of Porter. Rolph also served as secretary of the executive committee.

8. In addition to Torbitt, the nine members elected to the first finance committee included: P. H. Tapp, R. J. Menefee, John H. Leathers, John D. Taggart, Chas. W. Gheens, Dexter Hewitt, T. A. Lyon, and C. P. Atmore.

9. Within the interior cover pages of the UGM minute book, volume 1, is a newspaper clipping entitled "The Holcombe Mission, Once Under Methodist Management, Now Supported by All Evangelical Congregations" dated June, 1885.

10. Ibid.

11. Ibid.

12. Ibid.

13. Ibid., 15.

14. Maude M. Abner, *The Story of the Union Gospel Mission* (Louisville: Mayes Printing Company, 1944), 17-20, 141-150.

15. Ibid., 17.

16. Gross Alexander, *The Life and Work of Steve P. Holcombe: The Converted Gambler* (Louisville: Press of the Courier-Journal, 1888), 100-101.

17. Union Gospel Mission, volume 1, 16-17.

18. Ibid., 17, 250.

19. Steve P. Holcombe letter to S. P. Dalton, February 3, 1886. Printed in Alexander, *The Life and Work of Steve P. Holcombe: The Converted Gambler*, 99-100.

20. Union Gospel Mission, volume 1, 17-18.

21. Ibid., 22

22. Ibid., 23.

23. Ibid., 24, 31, 41, 45, 245.

24. Sam P. Jones letter to Hol*combe,* March 16, 1886. Published in Alexander,

The Life and Work of Steve P. Holcombe: The Converted Gambler, 166.

25. Union Gospel Mission, volume 1, 25-27.

26. Ibid., 25-31.

27. Union Gospel Mission, volume 1, 32-33.

28. Alexander, *The Life and Work of Steve P. Holcombe: The Converted Gambler,* 101.

29. Steve P. Holcombe letter to S. P. Dalton, April 17, 1886. Published in Alexander, *The Life and Work of Steve P. Holcombe: The Converted Gambler,* 138-139.

30. Standing committees included the already existing Executive Committee, Committee on Devotion, Committee on House and Grounds, Committee on Sunday School, and Committee on Industrial School.

31. Union Gospel Mission, volume 1, 35, 37.

32. Ibid., 34.

33. Ibid., 35.

34. Ibid., 35-36.

35. Ibid., 248. See May 20, 1886 letter of Rolph to Theo. Harris.

36. Ibid., 40.

37. Holcombe letter to S. P. Dalton, November 25, 1886. Published in Alexander, *The Life and Work of Steve P. Holcombe: The Converted Gambler,* 139.

38. Alexander, *The Life and Work of Steve P. Holcombe: The Converted Gambler,* 106.

39. Ibid., 107.

40. Union Gospel Mission, volume 1, 41, 43. On January 15, 1887, the directors authorized Holcombe to visit Chicago for the purpose of personally requesting Moody's assistance in raising funds.

41. Ibid., 45, 245.

42. Ibid., 49.

43. Martha King Alexander, *Seventy-Three Years of Kindergarten in Kentucky* (1938), 40. Mary Anne Fowlkes, "Kindergarten Movement" in *The Encyclopedia of Louisville* (The University Press of Kentucky, 2001), 483.

44. Union Gospel Mission, volume 1, 50.

45. Ibid.

46. For information on the Wayfarer's Rest, see Alexander, *The Life and Work of Steve P. Holcombe: The Converted Gambler,* 96-98.

47. Priest had served on the Committee of House and Grounds.

48. Union Gospel Mission, volume 1, 51.

49. Ibid., 52. Burghard briefly returned to the board of directors upon re-election at a September 6, 1890 meeting, although he soon accepted another position in New York; see Union Gospel Mission, volume 1, 69.

50. Alexander, *The Life and Work of Steve P. Holcombe: The Converted Gambler*, 120-121.
51. Union Gospel Mission, volume 1, 53.
52. Ibid., 57.
53. Ibid., 55, 244.
54. Ibid., 57-58.
55. Ibid., 59.
56. Ibid., 60.
57. Ibid., 63, 242.
58. Ibid., 64.

CHAPTER 4: THE HOLCOMBE LEGACY

1. Union Gospel Mission, volume 1, 65, [Manuscript documents relating to the Union Gospel Mission, Louisville, Ky.], Archives and Special Collections of the James P. Boyce Centennial Library, The Southern Baptist Theological Seminary, Louisville, Kentucky.
2. Ibid., 65-66.
3. Ibid., 66.
4. Ibid., 67.
5. Ibid., 68.
6. Ibid., 240.
7. Ibid., 69.
8. Ibid., 239.
9. Ibid., 71.
10. Ibid.
11. Ibid., 72.
12. Ibid., 74.
13. Ibid., 73.
14. Ibid., 74.
15. Ibid., 75.
16. Ibid., 76. Holcombe's daughter's name is alternatively rendered as "Mamie" in some documents and publications, including Alexander's *The Life and Work of Steve P. Holcombe: The Converted Gambler*. The "Mayme" spelling appears to have been preferred, however, as it is the one which adorns her gravestone near Elizabethtown, Kentucky.
17. Ibid.
18. Ibid., 25-26.
19. Maude M. Abner, *The Story of the Union Gospel Mission, 1886-1944* (Louisville: Mayes Printing Company, 1944), 40-41.
20. Union Gospel Mission, volume 1, 78.

21. Ibid., 79.

22. The extended statement: "The Board of Directors of the Union Gospel Mission and who have been in office since its inception desire before resigning their trust to—in justice to themselves and the general public who contributed the money necessary to start and equip the present mission—place on record in the minute book of the Mission, the fact that they continued the work of the Mission in full operation in all the branches of its work until by the lack of interest on the part of the public and the entire stoppage of contributions to support the preaching services this latter part of the work had to cease. That they paid the debt accruing up to that period by subscriptions from themselves and have since that time kept it free from debt—they furthermore have kept the other departments of work fully and efficiently maintained until now.

It has been the effort of the present Board from the beginning to encourage harmony in the different departments of the work and prevent as far as possible any conflict in the different kinds of work and to keep the corporation out of debt, so that the valuable property might be preserved for future good— and they feel that much good has resulted, and although for several years, the Board was unable to find and pay a suitable preacher the idea of having such a preacher was never abandoned and hopes were confidently entertained at a future time to resume this branch of the work. The Board carried on the Kindergarten work, the Mother's meeting Industrial School, and S. S. work and we have seen some of these branches of the work grow to very gratifying results and we are unanimously of opinion that there is abundant room in the present building now owned and used by the Union Gospel Mission for these and all the regular departments of the Mission work." Ibid., 80-81.

23. Josephus Pettus, George H. Simmons, J. Lithgow Smith, John Justi, George P. Kendrick, and P. M. Collier of the Holcombe Mission, were elected as the successors. S. P. Walker and W. S. Parker, had previously been elected as the first two successors of the Union Gospel Mission at the previous directors' meeting. Ibid., 79-82.

24. Ibid., 82.

25. Within the interior cover pages of the Mission minute book, volume 1, is a newspaper clipping entitled "The Holcombe Mission, Once Under Methodist Management, Now Supported by All Evangelical Congregations" dated June, 1885.

26. Ibid., 82.

27. Ibid., 83.

28. Ibid.

29. Ibid., 86, 187.

30. *First Annual Report of the Union Gospel Mission* (Louisville, John P. Morton

and Company, 1895), 6.

31. Ibid., 7.

32. Ibid., 8.

33. Ibid., 4.

34. Ibid., 4-5.

35. Union Gospel Mission, volume 1, 96, 163, 168.

36. Ibid., 163.

37. Frances Farley Gwinn, "Patty Smith Hill in Louisville" (M.A. thesis, University of Louisville, 1954), 131.

38. Union Gospel Mission, volume 1, 170, 172.

39. Ibid., 167.

40. Ibid., 205.

41. See Union Gospel Mission minutes, 1912, [undated typescript of Thos. D. Osborne address]. Maude Abner noted the directors' minutes from 1896-1906 were unavailable to her when she wrote the history of the Mission in 1944. *Abner, The Story of the Union Gospel Mission, 1886-1944*, 23.

42. Union Gospel Mission, volume 1, 195.

43. Ibid., 194.

44. Ibid., 195-198.

45. Abner, *The Story of the Union Gospel Mission, 1886-1944*, 42.

46. Ibid., 43.

47. In an 1886 letter to a friend, Holcombe wrote "Sister Clark is in her glory. She is one of the grandest Christian women I have ever seen." Published in Gross Alexander, *The Life and Work of Steve P. Holcombe: The Converted Gambler* (Louisville: Press of the Courier-Journal, 1888), 139.

48. Abner, *The Story of the Union Gospel Mission, 1886-1944*, 43.

49. Unattributed newspaper clipping dated 5 November, 1905 titled "Golden Anniversary. The Rev. Steve P. Holcombe and Wife Plan Celebration" glued into Union Gospel Mission, volume 1, 19.

50. Alexander, *The Life and Work of Steve P. Holcombe: The Converted Gambler,* 102. Unattributed newspaper clipping titled "Rev. and Mrs. Steve P. Holcombe" glued into Union Gospel Mission, volume 1, 10.

51. Union Gospel Mission, volume 1, 10, 19.

52. Ibid., 155-157.

53. Ibid., 158.

54. "Mission Passes: Steve Holcombe's Home for Destitute a Pioneer." *Courier-Journal,* 24 June 1906. Clipping is glued into the interior cover pages of the Union Gospel Mission, volume 1.

55. Ibid.

56. Undated and unattributed newspaper article titled "Holcombe Mission Trust-

ees to Meet: Mrs. Elizabeth Cardwell to Succeed Famous Founder July 1" glued into interior cover pages of the Union Gospel Mission, volume 1.

57. Ibid.

Chapter 5: New Fields for the Harvest

1. "Mission Passes: Steve Holcombe's Home for Destitute a Pioneer." *Courier-Journal*, 24 June 1906. Clipping is glued into the interior cover pages of the Union Gospel Mission minutes, volume 1, [Manuscript documents relating to the Union Gospel Mission, Louisville, Ky.], Archives and Special Collections of the James P. Boyce Centennial Library, The Southern Baptist Theological Seminary, Louisville, Kentucky.

2. Quoted from undated typescript of Thos. D. Osborne's address. Union Gospel Mission minutes, 1912.

3. "Mission Passes: Steve Holcombe's Home for Destitute a Pioneer."

4. Ibid.

5. Maude Abner wrote: "The services were conducted by various pastors and laymen, Mrs. Cardwell often giving the word when there was no other leader. Thus many men, women and children, were drawn away from sin to a nearness to Christ and many of them accepted Him as their personal Savior." Maude M. Abner, *The Story of the Union Gospel Mission, 1886-1944* (Louisville: Mayes Printing Company, 1944), 49.

6. "Mission Passes: Steve Holcombe's Home for Destitute a Pioneer."

7. When the Community Chest surveyed the work of the Mission in 1933, it specifically noted the organization's "day nursery for white children." See "Supplementary Report of the Union Gospel Mission" contained within Union Gospel Mission missions, 1933.

8. "Mission Passes: Steve Holcombe's Home for Destitute a Pioneer."

9. Cardwell is quoted in Abner, *The Story of the Union Gospel Mission, 1886-1944*, 45.

10. Ibid., 46, 71.

11. Referenced by Abner on page seven of her Jubilee Anniversary address "Past, Present, Future of the Union Gospel Mission," Union Gospel Mission minutes, 1935.

12. Abner, *The Story of the Union Gospel Mission, 1886-1944*, 50.

13. Ibid., 44. See also "The Holcombe Mission Has a Resident Tailor and Shoemaker." Unattributed newspaper clipping is glued onto a page of the Union Gospel Mission, volume 1, 19.

14. Abner, *The Story of the Union Gospel Mission, 1886-1944*, 46.

15. Union Gospel Mission minutes, 1907-1908, December 14, 1908.

16. Union Gospel Mission minutes, 1909, [undated circular letter].

17. "Union Gospel Mission Saw a Very Busy June." Unattributed newspaper clipping is glued into the interior cover pages of the Union Gospel Mission, volume 1.

18. Ibid.

19. Ibid.

20. The typescript of the minutes, signed by A. G. Renau, Secretary, misspelled the name as "Mr. S. Halcomb." Union Gospel Mission minutes, 1907-1908, January 8, 1908.

21. Ibid., April 9, 1908.

22. Ibid., April 27, 1908.

23. Ibid.

24. Ibid.

25. An undated typescript copy of the Mission's constitution is filed with the Union Gospel Mission minutes for the years of 1907 – 1908. This particular draft requires the Mission's board of managers to consist of twenty members "chosen as far as practical from the different Evangelical denominations, with not more than five from any one." Whether this copy's text reflects the 1908 amendments or a previous draft cannot be ascertained. It is clear that the Mission's board no longer aspired to include a participant from each evangelical congregation in Louisville, rather being content to encourage participation from members of each evangelical denomination.

26. Union Gospel Mission minutes, 1909, March 11, 1909 and April 15, 1909.

27. "Steve Holcombe Returns to Mission Harness Again." Unattributed newspaper clipping is glued into the interior cover pages of the Union Gospel Mission, volume 1.

28. "Day Nursery at Holcombe Mission." Unattributed newspaper clipping is glued into the interior cover pages of the Union Gospel Mission, volume 1.

29. Union Gospel Mission minutes, 1912, [undated typescript of Thos. D. Osborne address].

30. Osborne noted in his 1912 address that Louisville had become home to forty-seven benevolences endorsed by the Board of Trade and Commercial Club Committees, a crowded mission market when compared to the climate in which the Mission began in 1885. Ibid.

31. "Died in Mission That Was Life's Best Work" Unattributed newspaper clipping dated February 25, 1916 is glued onto pages 100-101 of the Union Gospel Mission, volume 1. See also untitled newspaper clipping glued onto page 99 of Union Gospel Mission, volume 1.

32. Ibid. See also: Abner, *The Story of the Union Gospel Mission, 1886-1944*, 37, 122.

33. Untitled newspaper clipping glued onto page 99 of Union Gospel

Mission, volume 1.

34. Union Gospel Mission minutes, 1917, June 11, 1917.

35. Cardwell to Osborne, June 18, 1917, Union Gospel Mission minutes, 1917.

36. Union Gospel Mission minutes, 1916, June 12, 1916.

37. Union Gospel Mission minutes, 1917, February 8, 1917.

38. Ibid. Abner, *The Story of the Union Gospel Mission, 1886-1944*, 47.

39. Union Gospel Mission minutes, 1917, March 8, 1917.

40. Ibid., October 4-11, 1917. Lillian C. Milanof, "Social Services/Education" in *The Encyclopedia of Louisville* (The University Press of Kentucky, 2001), 833.

41. Lillian C. Milanof, "Metro United Way" in *The Encyclopedia of Louisville* (The University Press of Kentucky, 2001), 617.

42. Union Gospel Mission minutes, 1918, "Report upon the Examination of the Books of the Account of the Union Gospel Mission."

43. Abner, *The Story of the Union Gospel Mission, 1886-1944*, 47-48.

44. Union Gospel Mission minutes, 1919, "Report upon the Examination of the Books of the Account of the Union Gospel Mission."

45. Documents are collected inside an envelope titled "Gheens Bequest" in Union Gospel Mission minutes, 1920.

46. Ibid.

47. Milanof, "Metro United Way" in *The Encyclopedia of Louisville* , 617.

48. David C. Liggett to W. E. Pilcher, January 12, 1927, Union Gospel Mission minutes, 1927.

49. Union Gospel Mission minutes, 1931, December 11, 1931.

50. Abner, *The Story of the Union Gospel Mission, 1886-1944*, 59.

51. Ibid., 52-58.

52. Union Gospel Mission minutes, 1932, February 12, 1932.

53. Abner, *The Story of the Union Gospel Mission, 1886-1944*, 71-72.

54. Ibid., 48.

55. "Supplementary Report of the Union Gospel Mission" contained within Union Gospel Mission missions, 1933.

56. Union Gospel Mission minutes, 1934, March 8, 1934. Hardwood floor installations in other rooms followed. Abner wrote: "I was not willing for her to have a room covered with linoleum while I had a hardwood floor, and as she had told me that she expected some day to make a gift of money to the Mission, and the Mission was not able to pay for the floor, I insisted that she use a part of her gift by having a hardwood floor put down. This she did and the Mission had the room painted. Our office secretary, Miss Ida Bayard, said she desired a hardwood floor, so she paid for hers." Abner, *The Story of the Union Gospel Mission, 1886-1944*, 71-72.

57. Abner, *The Story of the Union Gospel Mission, 1886-1944*, 72.

58. Union Gospel Mission minutes, 1934, September 14, 1934.
59. See "Service Reports" document included in Union Gospel Mission minutes, 1935.
60. Union Gospel Mission minutes, 1934, December 14, 1934.
61. Maude Abner to Mary Stotsenburg, January 28, 1936, Union Gospel Mission minutes, 1936.

CHAPTER 6: FROM LAMENTATIONS TO SERENDIPITY

1. Maude M. Abner, "Past, Present, Future of the Union Gospel Mission," Union Gospel Mission minutes, 1935, [Manuscript documents relating to the Union Gospel Mission, Louisville, Ky.], Archives and Special Collections of the James P. Boyce Centennial Library, The Southern Baptist Theological Seminary, Louisville, Kentucky.
2. Ibid.
3. Ibid.
4. Maude M. Abner, *The Story of the Union Gospel Mission, 1886-1944* (Louisville: Mayes Printing Company 1994), 68.
5. Abner, "Past, Present, Future of the Union Gospel Mission," 1935.
6. Union Gospel Mission minutes, March 13, 1936 and June 13, 1936.
7. Abner, *The Story of the Union Gospel Mission, 1886-1944*, 87.
8. Union Gospel Mission minutes, May 15, 1936. Abner, *The Story of the Union Gospel Mission, 1886-1944*, 85.
9. Union Gospel Mission minutes, August 22, 1935 and March 31, 1936. Abner, *The Story of the Union Gospel Mission, 1886-1944*, 87.
10. Union Gospel Mission minutes, March 12, 1937.
11. Abner, *The Story of the Union Gospel Mission, 1886-1944*, 88.
12. Union Gospel Mission minutes, December 12, 1936. Abner, *The Story of the Union Gospel Mission, 1886-1944*, 88.
13. Ibid.
14. Abner, *The Story of the Union Gospel Mission, 1886-1944*, 90-91. Union Gospel Mission minutes, February 4, 1937.
15. Abner, *The Story of the Union Gospel Mission, 1886-1944*, 94-95.
16. [Last Will and Testament of Elizabeth Montgomery Cardwell] in Union Gospel Mission minutes, 1937.
17. Union Gospel Mission minutes, January 14, 1938. Abner wrote about the welcoming impact with the sign had for visitors in Abner, *The Story of the Union Gospel Mission, 1886-1944*, 120-122. The gift came courtesy of Amelia Layer and Mrs. F. J. Schlomer in honor of their late mother.
18. Union Gospel Mission minutes, September 10, 1937.
19. Abner, *The Story of the Union Gospel Mission, 1886-1944*, 98.

20. Union Gospel Mission minutes, November 11, 1938 and December 9, 1938. Abner, *The Story of the Union Gospel Mission, 1886-1944*, 98-99.

21. Union Gospel Mission minutes, March 27, 1939. Abner, *The Story of the Union Gospel Mission, 1886-1944*, 104.

22. Union Gospel Mission minutes, June 16, 1939.

23. Ibid.

24. Union Gospel Mission minutes, June 9, 1939.

25. Union Gospel Mission minutes, June 22, 1939.

26. Abner recorded her account of the various discussions of proposals conducted by the Mission. Abner, *The Story of the Union Gospel Mission, 1886-1944*, 105-108.

27. Union Gospel Mission minutes, June 22, 1939.

28. Union Gospel Mission minutes, July 17, 1939.

29. Ibid.

30. The record states that O'Neal remarked: "We are out of the Chest, once and for all, and to forget them. We have money for a year's further work, and if we can't show the churches that we are needed, in that length of time, we ought to turn the property back to them." Ibid.

31. Ibid.

32. Abner to Herrman, August 11, 1939. Letter filed in Union Gospel Mission minutes, 1939.

33. Union Gospel Mission minutes, August 22, 1939.

34. Union Gospel Mission minutes, October 24, 1939.

35. Union Gospel Mission minutes, November 10, 1939 and November 17, 1939. The present size of the Board consisted of fourteen members (seven required for a quorum) while the constitution change increased its maximum size to twenty-five. This attempt did not succeed at enlarging the board's membership or in motivating the churches to greater involvement.

36. Ibid.

37. Union Gospel Mission minutes, November 22, 1939.

38. Abner, *The Story of the Union Gospel Mission, 1886-1944*, 108.

39. Ibid., 108-109.

40. Ibid. Union Gospel Mission minutes, February 9, 1940.

41. Union Gospel Mission minutes, May 17, 1940.

42. Abner, *The Story of the Union Gospel Mission, 1886-1944*, 110-111.

43. Union Gospel Mission minutes, June 7, 1940. Abner, *The Story of the Union Gospel Mission, 1886-1944*, 111.

44. Abner, *The Story of the Union Gospel Mission, 1886-1944*, 112.

45. Union Gospel Mission minutes, July 5, 1940. C. O. Ewing had served upon the Union Gospel Mission's board.

46. Union Gospel Mission minutes, July 5, 1940. Abner, *The Story of the Union Gospel Mission, 1886-1944*, 112.

CHAPTER 7: THE BAPTISTS' MISSION

1. Union Gospel Mission minutes, July 5, 1940, [Manuscript documents relating to the Union Gospel Mission, Louisville, Ky.], Archives and Special Collections of the James P. Boyce Centennial Library, The Southern Baptist Theological Seminary, Louisville, Kentucky.
2. Union Gospel Mission minutes, August 5, 1940.
3. Union Gospel Mission minutes, October 8, 1940.
4. Union Gospel Mission minutes, December 13, 1940.
5. Union Gospel Mission minutes, December 17, 1940.
6. Union Gospel Mission minutes, January 17, 1941.
7. Dallas Lee, *The Cotton Patch Evidence* (New York: Harper & Row, 1971), 21-22.
8. *Annual Session of the Long Run Association of Baptists in Kentucky* (1940), 13. Lee, *The Cotton Patch Evidence*, 22-23.
9. *Annual Session of the Long Run Association of Baptists in Kentucky* (1941), 13, 32. "Vacation Bible Schools," *The Hand of Fellowship*, 1 June 1941, p. 1. "U.G.M. Conducts Two Schools," *The Long Runner*, September 1941, p. 3.
10. Peter Smith, "The Story of Asenath Brewster: Pioneer in Urban Missions and Mentor of Southern Baptist Leaders," *Baptist History and Heritage* XLI (Winter 2006): 102-109.
11. *Annual Session of the Long Run Association of Baptists in Kentucky* (1941), 30-31.
12. Union Gospel Mission minutes, July 16, 1941 and August 29, 1941. *Annual Session of the Long Run Association of Baptists in Kentucky* (1941), 31-32.
13. "Mr. Barnett New Pastor at Gospel Mission," *The Long Runner*, 1 November 1941, p. 2.
14. Henlee H. Barnette, *Clarence Jordan: Turning Dreams into Deeds* (Smyth & Helwys, 1992), 2-3.
15. Ibid., 3-4.
16. Ibid., 5-6.
17. Henlee Hulix Barnette, *A Pilgrimage of Faith: My Story* (Macon: Mercer University Press, 2004), 55-56. Barnette met Charlotte Ford, a WMU Training School student who became his wife, when she began attending services at the Mission and eventually assumed the role of pianist.
18. *Annual Session of the Long Run Association of Baptists in Kentucky* (1941), 34.
19. *Annual Session of the Long Run Association of Baptists in Kentucky* (1941), 13.
20. Union Gospel Mission minutes, August 29, 1941 and January 20, 1942. "Union

Gospel Mission a Baptist Opportunity," *Western Recorder*, 13 February 1941, 16.

21. Union Gospel Mission minutes, September 22, 1941.

22. Maude M. Abner, *The Story of the Union Gospel Mission, 1886-1944* (Louisville: Mayes Printing Company, 1944), 135.

23. Union Gospel Mission minutes, June 1, 1942.

24. W. E. Pilcher to C. L. Jordan, June 4, 1942. Union Gospel Mission minutes, 1942.

25. W. Stuart Rule to W. E. Pilcher, June 19, 1942. Union Gospel Mission minutes, 1942. "Baptists Get Mission Property," *The Long Runner*, July 1942, p. 1-2.

26. *Annual Session of the Long Run Association of Baptists in Kentucky* (1942), 34.

27. Ibid.

28. "Union Gospel Mission Gets Special Worker," *The Long Runner*, March 1942, p. 1.

29. "Dr. Jordan Evangelist for U. G. M. Revival," *The Long Runner*, June 1942, p. 1-2. Barnette, *Clarence Jordan: Turning Dreams into Deeds*, 5.

30. Barnette, *Clarence Jordan: Turning Dreams into Deeds*, 5. James A. McCaleb, "Jordan to Quit Mission," *The Long Runner*, July 1942, p. 1-2.

31. Abner, *The Story of the Union Gospel Mission, 1886-1944*, 139.

32. Representing the interests of the various denominations connected with the Mission were E. J. Wells (Episcopal), Gene Sims (Methodist), W. Scott Miller (Christian), Junius C. Graves (Presbyterian), L. M. Render (Baptist), Alfred C. Kreiger (Evangelical and Reformed), and Lawrence F. Speckman (Lutheran). See copy of *Union Gospel Mission of Louisville vs. E. J. Wells, et. al.* in Union Gospel Mission minutes, 1943.

33. Ibid.

34. Union Gospel Mission minutes, September 23, 1943.

35. Barnette, *A Pilgrimage of Faith: My Story*, 59.

36. *Annual Session of the Long Run Association of Baptists in Kentucky* (1944), 19. J. Perry Carter, "Union Gospel Mission Changed to Central Baptist Mission," *Western Recorder*, 5 April 1945, p. 8.

37. Union Gospel Mission minutes, June 6 and July 13, 1944.

38. Union Gospel Mission minutes, July 13, 1944.

39. "The Story of the Union Gospel Mission," *The Long Run Baptist*, July 1951, 3.

40. Barnette, *A Pilgrimage of Faith: My Story*, 59.

41. James A. McCaleb, "Record Breaking Budget Adopted by Long Run," *The Long Runner*, December 1942, p.1

42. *Annual Session of the Long Run Association of Baptists in Kentucky* (1943), 33.

43. Ibid., 30.

44. *Annual Session of the Long Run Association of Baptists in Kentucky* (1944), 19.

45. *Annual Session of the Long Run Association of Baptists in Kentucky* (1943), 29.

46. "Central Baptist Mission Loses the Barnettes," *Western Recorder*, 13 September 1945, p10.

47. J. Perry Carter, "Union Gospel Mission Changed to Central Baptist Mission," *Western Recorder*, 5 April 1945, p. 8. *Annual Session of the Long Run Association of Baptists in Kentucky* (1944), 56.

48. "New Superintendent at Central Baptist Mission," *Western Recorder*, 18 October 1945, p. 10.

49. *Annual Session of the Long Run Association of Baptists* (1948), 28. *Annual Session of the Long Run Association of Baptists* (1949), 50.

50. *Annual Session of the Long Run Association of Baptists* (1951), 24.

51. Ibid., 25. "Central Baptist Mission," *The Long Run Baptist*, May 1952, p. 4.

52. Anita Roper, "Central Baptist Mission: Stories about Central Baptist Mission," *The Long Run Baptist*, April 1954, 4.

53. "Evangelism Emphasized at Central Baptist Mission," *The Long Run Baptist*, January 1950, 3.

54. *Annual Session of the Long Run Association of Baptists* (1956), 24. "Finley Ray, New Superintendent at Central Baptist Mission," *The Long Run Baptist*, July 1956, p. 3. "Bethel Mission to be Operated by Association," *The Long Run Baptist*, November, 1956, p. 4.

55. Between Sherman Towell's resignation in 1956 and Marvin Jackson's appointment in 1961, the succession of superintendents included Finley Ray, Walter Routh, and Ruben Speakman.

56. "Central Baptist Mission," *The Long Run Baptist*, October 1951, 4.

57. "Building Fund Begun for Central Baptist Mission," *The Long Run Baptist*, February 1954, 4.

58. "Relocation of Central Baptist Mission," *The Long Run Baptist*, April 1957, 1.

59. "Excellent Progress Made at Central Baptist Chapel," *The Long Run Baptist*, June 1958, p.1-2.

60. *Annual Session of the Long Run Association of Baptists* (1958), 43-44.

61. *Annual Session of the Long Run Association of Baptists* (1962), 37.

62. *Annual Session of the Long Run Association of Baptists* (1963), 7. "Central Baptist Chapel Building Bid Approved," *The Long Run Baptist*, June 1963, 1.

63. "Gracious Gift," *The Long Run Baptist*, February 1963, 1.

64. *Annual Session of the Long Run Association of Baptists* (1963), 40.

65. Ibid., 64-65.

66. Ibid., 79.

67. "Cornerstone Laying for the New Jefferson Street Baptist Church," *The Long Run Baptist*, October 1963, 3. "Calling All Baptists," *The Long Run Baptist*, April 1964, 1.

68. "Jefferson Street Baptist Chapel," *The Long Run Baptist*, May 1964, p. 1.

69. *Annual Session of the Long Run Association of Baptists* (1964), 54-55.

70. Ibid., 65, 91.

71. "Staff Changes," *Western Recorder*, 21 August 1971, p. 2.

72. Louisville Urban Renewal led to a spike in homelessness among African Americans in particular.

73. *Annual of the Long Run Baptist Association* (1971), 59-60. "Chapel Offers Help to Low Income Families," *Western Recorder*, 10 January 1970, p. 7.

CHAPTER 8: CHALLENGES OF THE MODERN ERA

1. Lowell Lawson, Bob Brackney, and William Fulkerson served in succession as the Center director between 1971 and 1979.

2. "Chapel Offers Help to Low Income Families," *Western Recorder*, 10 January 1970, p. 7.

3. *Annual of the Long Run Baptist Association* (1978), 59.

4. Larry High, "Senior Citizens Dine Out Five Days a Week," *Western Recorder*, 20 July 1974, p. 10.

5. *Annual of the Long Run Baptist Association* (1974), 40.

6. Ibid.

7. *Annual of the Long Run Baptist Association* (1975), 34.

8. *Annual of the Long Run Baptist Association* (1972), 40.

9. *Annual of the Long Run Baptist Association* (1975), 34.

10. *Annual of the Long Run Baptist Association* (1973), 61. *Annual of the Long Run Baptist Association* (1972), 40.

11. *Annual of the Long Run Baptist Association* (1979), 26.

12. Ibid., 25.

13. Ibid., 35.

14. *Annual of the Long Run Baptist Association* (1981), 20.

15. Ibid., 42.

16. Ibid., 43.

17. Ibid., *Annual of the Long Run Baptist Association* (1980), 35.

18. *Annual of the Long Run Baptist Association* (1983), 24-25, 52-53.

19. "Missionary Probe: William Michael Elliott," *Pioneer Probe* (July 1985), p. 29.

20. Ibid., 54.

21. *Annual of the Long Run Baptist Association* (1984), 59.

22. David Wilkinson, "Befriending the Homeless," *Light* (April 1986), 4.

23. *Annual of the Long Run Baptist Association* (1990), 27.

24. Wilkinson, "Befriending the Homeless," p. 5.

25. *Going for the Jugular: A Documentary History of the SBC Holy War*, ed. Walter B. Shurden and Randy Shepley (Mercer, 1996), 2-13.

26. Gregory A. Wills, *Southern Baptist Theological Seminary, 1859-2009* (Oxford University Press, 2009), 525.

27. *Going for the Jugular: A Documentary History of the SBC Holy War*, 92-93, 122-123.

28. Ibid., 124-134.

29. Wills, *Southern Baptist Theological Seminary, 1859-2009*, 527-539.

30. For records of all interactions between Cindy Weber and the Long Run Baptist Association, I am indebted to the records and correspondence housed in the personal papers of Cindy J. Weber in the offices of the Jeff Street Baptist Community at Liberty. These papers include correspondence sent and received by Weber, Bennett, Barry D. Dennis (JSBC Committee Chairman), Robert C. Jones (Director of Direct Missions Department, Kentucky Baptist Convention), Billy Craddock (Personnel Committee Chairman, LRBA), Harold W. Wilcox (association director of the Christian Social Ministries Centers Department, Home Mission Board), Dwight Lyons (Director of Mission and Ministries, LRBA), J. Anthony Hough (Director of Mission and Ministries, LRBA), Jim England (pastor of Deer Park Baptist Church), and Jim Holladay (pastor of East Baptist Church), between the years of 1987 and 1991.

31. Russell Bennett, "Heresy of Inerrancy," *Western Recorder*, 11 July 2000, p. 4.

32. Marv Knox, "Kentucky Moderates Decry Politicking, but Propose Slate," *Western Recorder*, 28 August 1990, p. 2.

33. Marv Knox, "Jeff Street Chapel to Vacate Building," *Western Recorder*, 15 October 1991, p. 9.

34. Cindy Weber to Russell Bennett, 2 March, 1989. [Records and personal papers of Cindy Weber, Jeff Street Baptist Community at Liberty]; *Annual of the Long Run Baptist Association* (1989), 1. The short-lived interim pastorate position was filled by two men in succession: Dan Aleshire and Jon Rainbow, neither of whom were officially members of the Jeff Street congregation, according to Weber.

35. Robert C. Jones to Russell Bennett, 4 November, 1888. [Records and personal papers of Cindy Weber, Jeff Street Baptist Community at Liberty].

36. Marv Knox, "Cindy Weber Installed at Jeff Street," *Western Recorder*, 3 September 1991, p. 2. *Annual of the Long Run Baptist Association* (1991), 43-44.

37. Knox, "Jeff Street Chapel to Vacate Building," p. 1, 9. *Annual of the Long Run Baptist Association* (1991), 43-44.

38. Knox, "Jeff Street Chapel to Vacate Building," p. 9. *Annual of the Long Run Baptist Association* (1991), 43-44.

39. *Annual of the Long Run Baptist Association* (1992), 20-21.

40. Ibid., 39. *Annual of the Long Run Baptist Association* (1995), 50a-50b.

41. *Annual of the Long Run Baptist Association* (1992), 20-21.

42. "Home Again in 18 Months," *Discovery* (February 1994), 8.

43. Ibid.

44. "Homeless Study Kicks Off Season of Missions," *Western Recorder*, 8 March 1994, p. 1.

45. Pat Cole, "Ministering to the Least of These," *Missions Today*, January 1998, p. 10-11.

46. Randall Harvey, "Jefferson Street Baptist Center," *The Colloquy*, 28 October 1996, p. 3.

47. *Annual of the Long Run Baptist Association* (1998), 56. Randall Harvey, "Report from Jefferson Street Baptist Center," *Colloquy*, 31 August 1996, p. 1.

48. Randall Harvey, "Jefferson Street Baptist Center," *The Colloquy*, 3 August 1998, p. 1. Ken Walker, "Center Proud of Return on Investment from Association," *Western Recorder*, 12 January 1999, p. 3.

49. *Annual of the Long Run Baptist Association* (1999), 62.

50. *Annual of the Long Run Baptist Association* (1997), 59. Walker, "Center Proud of Return on Investment from Association," p. 3.

51. *Annual of the Long Run Baptist Association* (2000), 30, 45.

52. David Winfrey, "New Homeless Ministry Tires to Help Men Get Back on Track," *Western Recorder*, 18 January 2000, p. 1.

53. *Annual of the Long Run Baptist Association* (2001), 83-84. *Annual of the Long Run Baptist Association* (2003), 50.

54. Ken Walker, "A Home, Sweet Home for Homeless," *Western Recorder*, 9 December 2003, p. 3.

55. Walker, "Center Proud of Return on Investment from Association," p. 3.

56. "Ministry Centers Leadership Update," *The Long Runner*, January 2003, p. 2.

57. Shirley Cox, "My Brother's Keeper, Missionary Brings Good News to Louisville's Homeless," *On Mission*, Special Issue 2007, 34.

58. Ibid., 35.

59. Ibid.

60. Drew Nichter, "Louisville's Jefferson Street Baptist Center Focuses on the Gospel in Serving City's Vast Homeless Community," *Western Recorder*, 24 November 2009, p. 3.

61. 24 CFR 576.23, accessed August 3, 2015, https://www.law.cornell.edu/cfr/text/24/576.23.

62. Bates expressed his position on the matter on his personal blog in an April 6, 2010 post appealing to the historical precedents of Roger Williams. Andrew Bates, "Teaching Baptists about their heritage of secular government," accessed August 3, 2015, https://chbcblog.wordpress.com/2010/04/06/teaching-baptists-about-their-heritage-of-secular-government/.

63. Nichter, "Louisville's Jefferson Street Baptist Center Focuses on the Gospel

in Serving City's Vast Homeless Community," 3.

64. Interview with Jesse Eubanks, 24 June 2015.

65. Ibid.

66. Interview with Bryce Butler, 18 June 2015.

67. Ruth Schenk, "Christmas Eve Brunch at Jefferson Street Baptist Center Lets the Homeless Know They Are Not Forgotten," *The Southeast Outlook*, 19 December 2012, accessed August 3, 2015, http://www.southeastoutlook.org/news/top_stories/article_c1103000-49f3-11e2-aeae-001a4bcf6878.html.

68. Wesley Kerrick, "Helping Hands Join Together," *The Voice-Tribune*, accessed August 3, 2015, http://www.voice-tribune.com/life-style-2/life-style-cover-stories/helping-hands-join-together/.

69. Interview with Bryce Butler, 18 June 2015.

70. *Jefferson Street Baptist Center 2012/2013 Annual Report*, accessed August 9, 2015, http://www.louisvillerescuemission.org/wp-content/uploads/2013/10/Jefferson-Street-Baptist-Center-2012-2013-Annual-Report-Website.pdf.

71. The legal name remained Jefferson Street Baptist Center, Inc. Bryce Butler shared a copy of this letter dated November 22, 2013.

72. Louisville Rescue Mission, Accessed June 10, 2015, http://www.louisvillerescuemission.org/.

Epilogue

1. Ruth Schenk, "Louisville Rescue Mission Makes Total Life Change Goal for Every Client," *The Southeast Outlook*, 4 December 2014, p. 8. Claire Galofaro, "Volunteers Count Homeless in National Initiative," *Courier-Journal*, 30 January 2015, accessed August 9, 2015, http://www.courier-journal.com/story/news/local/2015/01/29/coalition-homeless-conducts-annual-count-people-living-louisville-streets/22518025/.

Steve P. Holcombe.

Steve P. Holcombe established his Gospel Mission in 1881 and became well known in Louisville by 1888 when his first biography saw publication.

BIRTHPLACE OF MR. HOLCOMBE, SHIPPINGSPORT.

MRS. S. P. HOLCOMBE.

THE OLD MILL AT SHIPPINGSPORT.

Holcombe learned to gamble and love in Shippingport. As a boy, he fished for petty fodder around the mill. As a young man, he married Mary Evans, the only woman who held affection for him.

A NIGHT MEETING—MR. HOLCOMBE PREACHING.

ENGINE HOUSE.

Holcombe worked long hours at a Louisville fire engine house before starting the Mission, where he preached to large crowds. *Bottom right:* Gross Alexander was the Methodist minister who led Holcombe to Christ and discipled him in the early years after his conversion.

JAMES WILLIAMS
AS HE WAS.

JAMES WILLIAMS
AS HE IS.

James Williams was a degenerate drunkard known as "Whiskey Jim" before conversion under Holcombe's preaching. The Walnut Street Methodist Church was the first congregation to support Holcombe's Mission.

THE INDUSTRIAL SCHOOL.

KINDERGARTEN.

Holcombe and the Union Gospel Mission provided a multitude of charitable services to the city's destitute, including one of America's most successful kindergarten schools. The Wayfarer's Rest provided sanctuary and work for men while the Industrial School taught sewing and tailoring to women and children.

THE WAYFARER'S REST.

1. EXTERIOR.   2. OFFICE.   3. SLEEPING APARTMENT.   4. TAKING MEALS.   5. AT WORK.   6. ON THE LEVEE.

THE UNION GOSPEL MISSION.

The Mission secured permanent housing in 1887 at a historic mansion on Jefferson Street. Mrs. J. M. Clark was the Mission's first kindergarten superintendent.

Opposite: The Union Gospel Mission's original constitution was ratified on April 18, 1885.

MRS. J. M. CLARK.

April 18/85

Pursuant to Adjournment & to call
the following named parties met at
8 o'clock pm at Y. M. C. a, Room

J. P. Corbitt, Geo Wilborn, C. T. Atmore
Frank Miller, Christ McClure, Jno L
Wheat, Jno Y Carter, Jno A Carter,
A Bell Cea, H. V. Loving, D. A. Tapp
Jno D Taggart, Jno Chilton, J Smith
Fred L. Richardson, R J Menefee
W. T. Ralph, J. T. Zurgheard

Proceedings opened by prayer

The Com to whom was referred the
Constitution reported & on motion the
Same was read Section by Section &
was adopted as a whole — The
following is the Constitution

Constitution

Name

The name of the organization
Shall be The Union Gospel
Mission of Louisville Ky

Object —

The object shall be to do
General Gospel City Missionary
work to reach the masses
who are without Gospel privileges
and to provide for the wants
of those who need Christian
teaching & encouragement

Teaching —

The management and
teaching shall be strictly evan-
-gelical and absolutely non-
-denominational

Shall be Controlled by a Board
of Managers — The control of

Steve Holcombe resigned from the Mission in 1889, returned in 1893 and served until his retirement in 1906, one month before his seventy-first birthday.

SUNDAY SCHOOL NOVEMBER 3, 1935
Golden Jubilee Year

Elizabeth M. Cardwell
succeeded Holcombe
and shifted the Mission's
focus into a day nursery
for children.

Maude M. Abner succeeded Cardwell
as Mission superintendent in 1933.
By the 1940s, the Mission's mansion
had degraded and required substantial
property maintenance.

Opposite: The Mission's Board of
Directors sought assistance from
Southern Baptists as finances dwindled.

BOARD MEMBERS 1935

BOARD MEMBERS 1940

CALLING ALL BAPTISTS

DEDICATION AND OPEN HOUSE
May 3, 1964 - 2:30 to 5:00 P.M.

"Come and See"

is the devotional theme for the Season of Prayer for associational missions in May. On this happy occasion we cordially invite all the members of the churches in Long Run Association to "Come and See" what Baptists have wrought in this strategic downtown community.

The dedication service will begin at 2:30 and Open House from 3:30 to 5:00 P.M.

In the 1940s, the Long Run Baptist Association rescued the Mission from ruin due to the missionary leadership of Clarence Jordan *(top left)* and Henlee Barnette *(middle left and bottom right)*. Southern Baptists built a new facility on Jefferson Street in 1964.

Sherman Towell led the Mission through a decade of growth and implemented creative outreach strategies. Under Marvin Jackson *(opposite, bottom left)*, the Mission expanded its social services and promoted racial reconciliation.

OF WAGONS, OUT-OF-DOORS, AND GOD!

Jefferson Street Baptist Chapel, Long Run Baptist Association's old and historic mission center, has concluded one of its most successful summer programs in its history. One of the keys to its success was an aggressive outreach into the Clarksdale community, six square blocks of public housing which is the prime neighborhood served by the Chapel.

During the early weeks of summer the Chapel sent a fleet of Godwagons into the community each morning to establish four combination-playground-Vacation Bible Schools. As many as 135 children were reached each morning.

The Mission provided many opportunities for children to learn, play, and serve their community.

Ministry To Downtown Multitudes

Childrens' Group

BOLD ASSOCIATIONAL MINISTRIES
May 18-25

FRED TUCKER SEASON OF PRAYER
FOR ASSOCIATIONAL MISSIONS
Offering Goal $15,000 for Long Run Baptist Associational Missions

WEEK OF PRAYER
FOR
Associational Missions
May 15-20, 1961

Long Run Association of Baptists

LOVE
SHARES

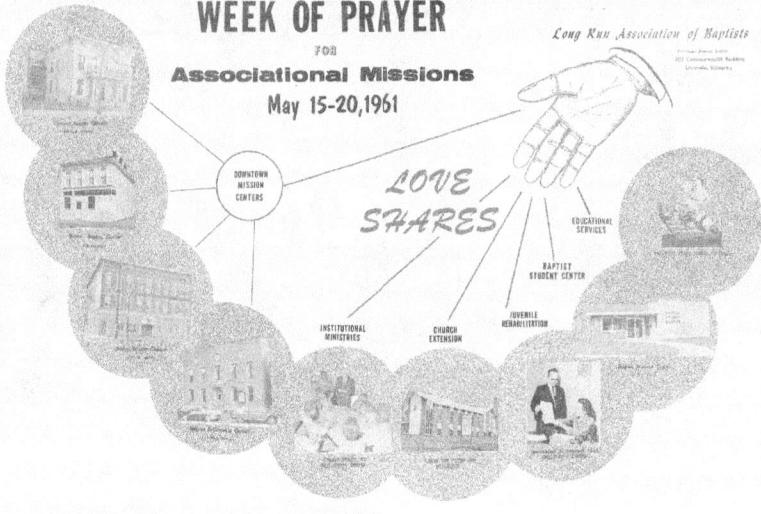

The Long Run Baptist Association heavily promoted the Mission and its other ministries through financial offerings and prayer weeks.

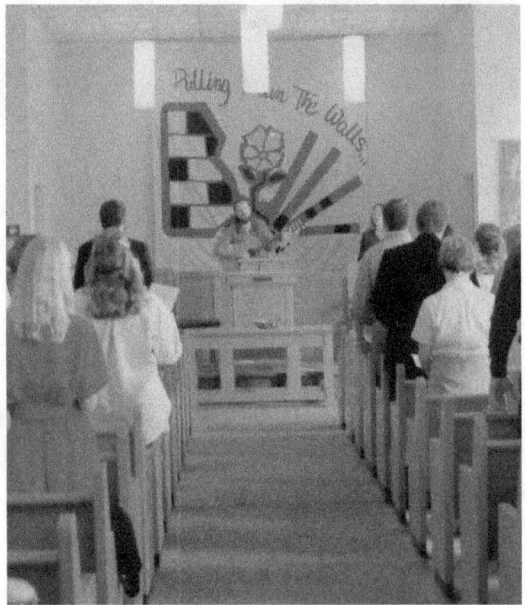

During the 1980s,
Michael Elliott *(top
left)* and Cindy Weber
(middle right) focused
on homeless ministry.
Weber clashed with LRBA
executive director Russell
Bennett *(middle left)*
over her growing pastoral
involvement, resulting in
a 1991 split.

Photo credits: Cindy J. Weber, *Light* (April 1986)

Construction of the Mission's current center in the 1960s *(left)*; Former Mission directors Randall Harvey *(directly below)* and Phil Schultz *(middle left)*.

In the 21st century, the Mission has expanded its homeless ministries and renewed its evangelical commitment. Bryce Butler *(bottom)* received the Holcombe Mercy Ministry Award in 2015 for his leadership in fundraising.

Today, the Mission offers aid services for residents and visitors. Worship services are provided on a weekly basis through preachers from local churches, Southern Seminary, and Baptist mission boards.

Dedicated staff like Joanie Williams *(top left)* and volunteers serve the physical and spiritual needs of the homeless.

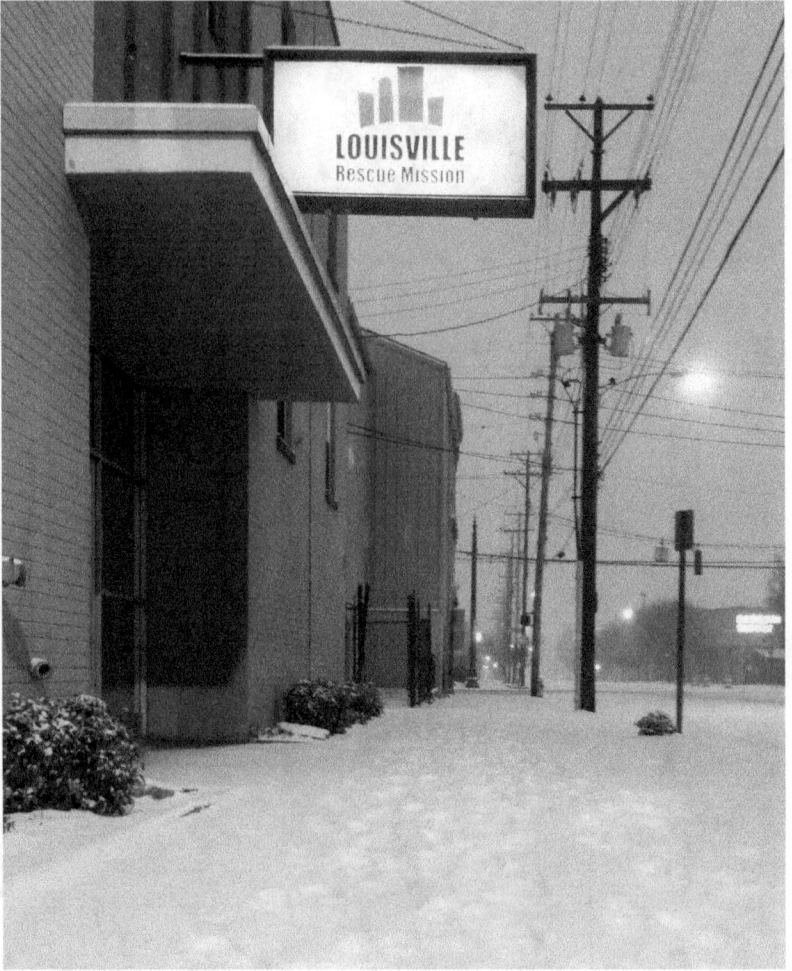

Additional photo credits: Louisville Rescue Mission; Archives and Special Collections, James P. Boyce Centennial Library, The Southern Baptist Theological Seminary, Louisville, Kentucky; The Ethics and Religious Liberty Commission of the Southern Baptist Convention; Cindy J. Weber; Long Run Baptist Association; Gross Alexander, _Steve P. Holcombe, The Converted Gambler, His Life and Work_ (1888); Maude M. Abner, _The Story of the Union Gospel Mission_ (1944)